Sanctified Living

Other books in the Lutheran Voices series

Sanctified Living

More than Grace and Forgiveness

Frank G. Honeycutt

Augsburg Fortress

Minneapolis

SANCTIFIED LIVING
More than Grace and Forgiveness

Library of Congress Cataloging-in-Publication Data
Honeycutt, Frank G., 1957–
  Sanctified living : more than grace and forgiveness / Frank G. Honeycutt.
      p. cm. — (Lutheran voices)
  Includes bibliographical references.
  ISBN 978-0-8066-8011-8 (alk. paper)
  1. Lutheran Church—Doctrines. 2. Sanctification. 3. Justification (Christian theology)
  I. Title.

  BX8065.3.H66 2008
  234'.8—dc22   2008000979

Purchases of ten or more copies of this book are available at a discount from the publisher.
For more information, contact the sales department at Augsburg Fortress, Publishers, 1-800-
328-4648, or write to: Sales Director, Augsburg Fortress, Publishers, Box 1209, Minneapolis,
MN 55440-1209.

12   11   10   09   08   1   2   3   4   5   6   7   8   9   10

For Pastor Mark Graham, Roanoke, Virginia—
Friend and conversation partner in matters
of sanctification and discipleship
for twenty-five years

Contents

Introduction

I know, O Lord, that the way of human beings is not in their control, that mortals as they walk cannot direct their steps. Correct me, O Lord, but in just measure; not in your anger, or you will bring me to nothing.

—Jeremiah 10:23-24

In one of my former parishes there was a difficult woman, now deceased, whom I will call Bernice. Over time, I came to doubt Bernice's excuse that she was too old and sick to attend worship on Sunday mornings, especially after bumping into her at Eckerd's during the week, out in her baby blue Cadillac "to pick up a few things." Even so, dutifully, I would drive the eight miles to her house with my portable home communion kit on the first Thursday of each month and offer the Lord's body and blood in her cramped den.

A large-screen television, almost brushing the ceiling and reporting the world's relentless woes, threw a dancing glow upon Bernice's collection of hundreds of ceramic dwarves that she arranged in a miniature city. They filled almost every available flat surface in the room—a table served as the main town commons where most of the small citizens resided, an ottoman housed several of the suburbanites, and a narrow lamp stand functioned as a handy elevated resort area.

I don't know how else to say this politely, but Bernice—a large woman with a hankering for Little Debbie Swiss Cake Rolls (the factory was only a couple hours away in Tennessee)—had the eyes and nostrils of a wild horse, like the several that roamed free in the highlands just north of town. I've never been at ease around horses, even though most of my ministry has been located in rural Virginia where many of my church members work on old family farms, some deeded by Lord Fairfax himself. Yet, I have this recurring dream where I'm trapped behind a horse that's about to wallop me squarely in the jaw with her agitated hindquarters and there is no time to get out of the way.

Bernice always began a conversation so abruptly that one needed a few moments to catch up and join her train of thought. One Thursday, as I stood on the front steps with my cradled communion kit and Bible, even before the first hello I heard an urgent question through the screen door: "Well, did you hear about the little princess?" Sitting across the alley on his front porch, a neighbor looked over the top of a newspaper, ears attuned to a voice that could easily carry across several town blocks. Bernice was forever offering such lightning bolts out of the blue. One poor member of our parish shared how he once picked up the phone in his wife's hospital room late the same night after her radical mastectomy and heard a loud raspy voice ask, "Well, did they take the whole breast, Ed?" No one had to tell Ed who was on the other end of the line—no identification needed.

This time, her obsession centered upon the sad case of Jon-Benet Ramsey, the little six-year-old beauty queen found murdered mysteriously on the day after Christmas in the basement of her parents' Colorado home. I'd not heard the latest. Now on the threshold in the sunshine, Bernice's fiery gaze angled downward from a height that resembled a pulpit. She glared as if her pastor had just stepped off another planet, announcing to anyone within earshot, "They found some semen, you know!"

With a sideways glance, I noticed the man across the alley had gone inside. A television commercial behind Bernice's door declared the goodness of maize. She spoke with the zeal of a prophet, as if I personally could do something right that moment concerning the immediate incarceration of a criminal several states away. I was certain this obsession for swift justice easily overshadowed the real presence of Jesus, shared momentarily amidst the ceramic throng, in any sort of practical relevance.

Her strident sermon that day helped recall another impromptu visit to Bernice's village of dwarves. In the first autumn following my arrival in the mountains, an older member of the congregation, a man I'd hardly had time to meet, died one afternoon in a tractor accident, crushed under the weight of machinery that had replaced harnessed horses several generations before. On the way home from meeting with the grieving family, I swung by Bernice's to ask a few questions about the deceased—biographical fodder for a funeral homily. She'd known the man since childhood. "He deserves death," was her candid response to my pastoral fishing. I was speechless. "He married beneath himself." Her eyes danced menacingly, refusing to back down, daring me to disagree. Bernice regularly reminded me of Ruby Turpin, a character in the classic Flannery O'Connor short story, *Revelation*.

> Sometimes Mrs. Turpin occupied herself at night naming the classes of people. On the bottom of the heap were most colored people, not the kind she would have been if she had been one, but most of them; then next to them—not above, just away from—were the white trash; then above them were the homeowners, and above them the home-and-land owners, to which she and Claud belonged. Above she and Claud were people with a lot of money and much bigger houses and much more land.[1]

In the final spring of her life, forty days after Easter, on Ascension Thursday, I visited Bernice for the last time, tucking the communion wafers and wine into the only available corner of her den table. One of the small figurines seemed to resemble Jesus, arms upraised, feeding the hungry multitude. We shared the holy elements and then prayed together. She always prayed with eyes wide open. "I feel so clean," she confided after communion, nostrils flared for emphasis, "like I've just stepped out of the shower." I heard a faint whinny in the nearby pasture.

It was raining that afternoon as I drove back to the church. I noticed spring peepers coming alive in the river that ran beside the road, the river that sometimes overflowed its banks that time of year, spilling into and blocking the spare traffic passing through town. The phone rang at home the Saturday night before Pentecost Sunday. Bernice had died. She was no longer bound to her ample body that filled her very crowded den.

Bernice was an especially trying child of God. She's among just a handful of parishioners I've ever wanted to slap. But on that Thursday afternoon, sharing communion among her ceramic city of dwarves, I was also reminded (again) of my own various and sundry shortcomings. We all deserve death. Upon realizing this for the first or 500th time, something like scales fall from our eyes and we see his arms upraised in blessing, our sins small and large washed clean by the blood of Jesus, the man of grace forever wedded to this world well beneath himself.

In almost twenty-five years as a pastor, I've noticed that it is very difficult for Lutherans to talk about sanctification—growth in the Holy Spirit, actual progress and maturity in the Christian life. We have a wonderful theology of grace and forgiveness. Our church was born in a spiritual context of rigid legalism and "works righteousness," faithfully and forcefully exposed by Martin Luther and the reformers. There is still a great need to proclaim unconditional grace in a culture bent on revenge and the almost gleeful ranking of certain sins. We can never be good enough to earn the love of Christ or bad enough to fall outside the wide net of his care, of his clear invitation to repentance. Creative proclamation of this message is as urgent in the twenty-first century as it was in the sixteenth. Lutherans are rightfully wary of any spiritual improvement program that attempts to ascend into some rarefied air of pious superiority where God surely smiles more on those earning special brownie points of goodness and achievement—God's halo children.

But after serving as pastor in a variety of settings (rural, small town, urban), I've also noticed that our historic commitment to this sound Reformation teaching that countered past spiritual abuses often makes us latter-day Lutherans quite nervous—even agitated and combative—when hearing words like *holiness* or *conversion* or even *growth*. With what language and teaching does the church confront a long-time parishioner like Bernice without sounding like a raving fundamentalist? She was certainly a forgiven sinner, cleansed by the gift of the sacraments. But how can someone as frustrating and judgmental as Bernice change and grow in Christ over time? Indeed, how can I?

We live in an American religious context in which, on any given Sunday, fully two-thirds of all ELCA church members are absent from worship, cut off from the life-giving power of God's word and sacraments. Sunday has become another Saturday for many Lutheran households. Basic core habits and spiritual disciplines assumed by our forebears are regularly ignored by the majority of people affiliated with our congregations. Martin Luther faced similar concerns and stated them forcefully in his "Preface" to *The Large Catechism*. The following quotation (a vibrant call to return to the practice of regular spiritual practices taught and arranged in the catechism) reveals Luther's conviction that grace can be misunderstood as anything goes: "In this way [pastors] would once again show honor and respect to the gospel, through which they have been delivered from so many burdens and troubles, and they might feel a little shame that, like pigs and dogs, they are remembering no more of the gospel than this rotten, pernicious, shameful, carnal liberty."[2] I find it amusing that we who raise red flags of legalism and works righteousness when discussing issues of sanctification forget that Luther urged daily prayers (centered in the Lord's Prayer) for children at least five times per day: "Until they recite them they should be given nothing to eat or drink."[3] I'm not suggesting we follow Luther's advice here, but do find our modern (and nervous) approach to issues of sanctification rather laughable given Luther's historic forcefulness.

I sometimes feel like a hired chaplain, called to serve the stated and felt religious "needs" of parishioners whenever such needs happen to arise—which is to say, in terms defined by the individual. How do Lutheran pastors, teachers, leaders, and parents address this spiritual reality without compromising our historic affirmations and convictions concerning grace and forgiveness?

Barbara Brown Taylor, popular writer and preacher in the Episcopal tradition, tells of a Lebanese seminary student who brought a memorable charge against his North American classmates one day: "All you Americans care about is justification! You love sinning and being forgiven, sinning and being forgiven, but no one seems to want off that hamster wheel. Have you ever heard of sanctification? Is anyone interested in learning to sin a little less?"[4]

That student's question serves as a prompt for the thesis of this book: there *is* a theology of sanctification for our church that avoids the pitfalls of smug sanctimony on the one hand and cheap grace on the other. Lutherans do not have a very developed theology of sanctification (in contrast to the advent of Methodism when the Wesley brothers were obsessed with the topic). The late and influential Lutheran theologian Gerhard Forde is fairly suspicious about the whole enterprise: "Sanctification, if it is to be spoken of as something other than justification, is perhaps best defined as the art of getting used to unconditional justification wrought by the grace of God for Jesus' sake.... Sanctification is a matter of being grasped by the unconditional grace of God and having now to live in that light."[5]

Our Lutheran history is grounded in a time when the clarion call of justification by grace through faith was the pressing gospel message of the day. But images and stories of sanctification and the relentless, life-changing power of the Holy Spirit also fill the pages of Holy Scripture (which is why I will be referring more to the Bible in this book than to the reformers). "Do not be so confident of forgiveness," says one of the writers of the Apocrypha, "that you add sin to sin" (Sir 5:5). Over time, even Lutherans can grow in holiness and indeed learn how to sin a little less.

1

Baptized into His Death

On the way, at a place where they spent the night, the Lord met Moses and tried to kill him.

—Exodus 4:24

On that great and glorious day in the future when I meet Christ face-to-face, there are several questions I plan to ask about various stories in the Bible. For one, what's with that tale about the angry she-bears who mauled forty-two young boys whose chief sin seems to be the rather innocent impertinence of calling God's prophet a name (2 Kings 2:23-24)? *Yikes.* Can't we teach the lads a lesson some other way? Or how about the strange vow of Jephthah the Gileadite whose obsession with victory against his enemies was so intense that he promised to sacrifice the first person exiting his back door if only God would grant him success in battle? Too bad for the daughter who met him dancing for joy that day, but a vow's a vow, and there was no "balm in Gilead" for her. Dad granted the lass two months to "wander on the mountains" and mourn her virginity with her friends. At the end of that hike, the promise stood (Judg. 11:29-40). I also plan to ask Jesus about his rather bizarre counsel concerning castration and remaining single (Matt. 19:10-12). "Let anyone accept this who can," he says. Never noticed many lining up for this teaching in the congregations I've served.

These strange stories, however, are easily eclipsed by God's attempt to kill Moses in the wilderness after our hero finally agrees to sign on and stand up to Pharaoh. Have you ever noticed this? Moses offers excuse after excuse to the God of the burning bush who needs a human voice to confront Egyptian power. The fourth chapter of Exodus catalogs some fairly good reasons why Moses is certain that God's got the wrong guy. Among them: "I am slow of speech and slow of tongue" (Exod. 4:10). Moses drags his feet but finally heads south on his mission and settles into camp for the night only to be jumped by God, who tries to kill him (4:24). Only the quick thinking of Zipporah, Moses' faithful wife, saves the day. She cuts off her son's foreskin, rubs her husband's feet with the bloody mess, and seems to send God packing: "So [God] let [Moses] alone" (4:26). I've asked several pastors and theologians what this text could possibly mean. One replied, "You just don't mess with The Big Guy." Yikes, indeed.

But I've become rather fond of a possible foreshadowing in this old, strange story that seems to parallel our theology of Holy Baptism. "What then is the significance of such a baptism with water?" asks Luther in *The Small Catechism* (1529). "Answer: It signifies that the old creature in us with all sins and evil desires is to be drowned and die through daily contrition and repentance, and on the other hand that daily a new person is to come forth and rise up to live before God in righteousness and purity forever."[1] Luther cites Romans 6:4 as the scriptural basis for this watery death: "Therefore we have been buried with him by baptism into death, so that, just as Christ was raised from the dead by the glory of the Father, so we too might walk in newness of life." But others could be quoted as well: "I want to know Christ and the power of his resurrection and the sharing of his sufferings by becoming like him in his death" (Phil. 3:10); "When you were buried with [Christ] in baptism, you were also raised with him through faith in the power of God, who raised him from the dead" (Col. 2:12); "Set your minds on things that are above, not on things that are on earth, for you have died, and your life is hidden with Christ in God" (Col. 3:2-3); and "I have been crucified with Christ; and it is no longer I who live, but it is Christ who lives in me" (Gal. 2:19-20).

It's a difficult theological twist to explain to new parents who will soon hold a beautiful baby at a font, with smiles and camera flashes, but in baptism God seeks to drown us and create a whole new person. God not only jumped poor Moses in the wilderness and "tried to kill him." In Holy Baptism, God jumps all his children and actually does. The circumcised foreskin waved by Zipporah thwarts a murderous God in Exodus. In baptism (the spiritual replacement of circumcision for the Christian), we have no such luck.

On baptismal Sundays in certain areas of Central America, the priest enters a somber congregation who gather to sing funeral hymns. A father carrying a small coffin and mother carrying the baby follow the priest to the altar. Ample water fills the wooden box, poured slowly in thanksgiving. The priest plunges the child into the water with the words, "I kill you in the name of the Father, Son, and Holy Spirit." Nobody moves. "And I raise you to live with the resurrected Lord forever." The congregation breaks into joyful song. I'm the first to admit that such a practice here in North America would quickly grab the attention of the local department of social services. But it does get this much right: *baptism is a death*. As someone once put it, "Baptism is both tomb and womb." We die with Christ and God raises us to live with him forever.

One of the things that is missing in many Lutheran congregations (and thereby stunting any notion of growth and sanctification in the Christian life that follows) is this whole notion of death and resurrection in the sacrament of holy baptism. "That baby can't die. She's just too cute!" And so baptism becomes a rite of passage, a family tradition, or, worse yet, some sort of special insurance against all evil and mishap. I've always found this latter belief rather ironic since Jesus goes straight from his baptism, almost dripping wet, directly to an encounter with the devil in the wilderness.[2] Instead of "protecting" Jesus from evil, baptism seems to hasten his encounter with such.

The celebration of our earthly birthdays, the moment of bambino appearance through human parents, usually far surpasses any baptismal anniversary remembrance in relative size or importance. Why do Christians pull out all the stops on birthdays and largely have no idea when they died and rose in the waters with Christ? I am convinced that until churches celebrate our baptismal "death date" into the body of Christ at least as vigorously as our planetary birth dates, then the potential for change and transformation in the church will be overshadowed by the regular glorification of the individual.

Some congregations that still have cemeteries attached to the church building employ a powerful practice that underscores this important connection between baptism and death. After the baptism of a child or adult, the entire congregation processes to the adjacent cemetery where the baptismal water used in worship that morning is then poured directly onto the gravesite where the body of the newly baptized will one day reside after they have breathed their last. This is not a morbid event but rather a bold proclamation that the person has *already died* in the waters and now swims in the abiding grace of God no matter what this life may hold in the future.

Once we get straight that a death has occurred in baptism, the church can recover how God then brings new life to all the baptized washed up on a Red Sea shore. We have crossed over. William Stringfellow, the renowned American lay theologian who died in 1985, reflected upon the Holy Spirit's gift of sanctification:

> [I]t does not mean being otherworldly, but it means being deeply implicated in the practical existence of this world without succumbing to this world or any aspect of this world, no matter how beguiling. Being holy means a radical self-knowledge; a sense of who one is, a consciousness of one's identity so thorough that it is no longer confused with the identities of others, of persons or of any creatures or of God or of any idols. . . . [I]n becoming and being sanctified, *every* facet, feature, attribute, and detail of a person is exposed and rejuvenated, rendered new as if in its original condition again, and restored.[3]

Stringfellow went on to give the example that the incredible zeal of Paul, once used to harass and persecute Christians, is now used (post-baptism) to zealously spread the gospel with surpassing tenacity. Such a tendency in Paul's identity was not eliminated or even suppressed by his baptism but instead utterly transformed for a new purpose as he appears before folk ranging from jailers to emperors with the truth of the gospel. This is the Holy Spirit's intent in sanctification: not to create some super-Christian but rather to transform in a person what God has already created. This is why I think it's wrong-headed to tell youth and children that they "can be anything they want to be" in adulthood. We *cannot* be just anything we choose if God creates us with unique gifts that are now transformed for kingdom purposes. Telling children something else is a theological lie. The emergence of such a radical understanding of our identity begins by confessing, "I have died with Christ. It is no longer I who am alive but Christ alive within me."

Why Many Christians Only Dabble in the Bible

There was a time in my early pastoral life that I believed people failed to read the Bible with any consistent regularity because we were all such busy people. There just was not enough time in the day. Running hither and yon, we never got around to the Word of God because of the frantic pace of our culture. Some important things had to go and the Bible became one of them because, well, we are a busy bunch with vital things to do. I'm not being cynical here. I really believed that once upon a time.

However, I do not believe it anymore. To put it more precisely, I don't believe that's the *primary* reason we fail to read the book. Here's what I've come to believe deep in my pastoral heart. Many people, even active, church-going Christians, do not read the Bible with any regularity *because we're afraid of what we might find there.*

All of us, pastors included, have a list of our favorite Bible passages—our own personal biblical canon. For Lutherans, that usually includes the Christmas story, a few favorite parables about lost sons and passersby on the other side of the road, a smattering of psalms, and key passages from Romans. The Bible, however, has an agenda beyond what we deem as our "favorite passages" and stories that affirm and comfort, bless and bring hope. A huge chunk of the Bible means to change us, to transform us more and more into the likeness of Jesus, to *convert* us, using a term that isn't found in many Lutheran circles.

This, I've come to believe, is why many do not read the Bible with any regularity. Because what we read there compared to how we choose to arrange our lives is often just too much to bear or think about. So we settle for affirmation and blessing. Don't get me wrong—we need large doses of both. But we also, deep down, need a word that cuts away the multitude of rationalizations, my adept penchant for avoidance. In short, the Bible invites us to die, to view this life from God's perspective rather than through our own narrow lens. And frankly this is a lot of hard, exhausting work. And so we settle for snippets rather than the whole story. Someone once said that baptism in the modern church is often like the old Brylcreem commercial: "a little dab will do ya."

We recently had a family leave the congregation because our church council refused to allow a baptism under the terms they were requesting—privately, apart from Sunday morning and the worshiping body; a retired clergy relative presiding; no clear connection to any congregation for the parents or child (all of whom lived many miles away). When asked why the baptism had to occur in such a fashion, the consistent answer was, "We just want to have it done our way." I applauded our council for making a courageous decision, knowing that this family was likely to exit when they didn't get their way. It is difficult for us to speak the truth in love in church. We're used to giving people what they want, reflecting a society where the consumer is king. "Have I now become your enemy by telling you the truth?" asks Saint Paul of the church in Galatia (4:16).

Writing about evangelism in a new century, Bryan Stone, a new and provocative United Methodist voice articulating faithful Christian witness in North America, suggests that we are in a period very similar to the early church:

> As Tertullian insisted, people are "made, not born, Christians," and we know that by at least the third century, the process of making Christians could take up to three years. Given the intense and ongoing culture of conversion within which we live today, there is no reason to believe that conversion to Christianity will take place any faster. Indeed, there is every reason to believe that the process will resemble an intensive and sustained process of detoxification.[4]

So let me restate what I've come to believe. I believe we've largely stopped reading the Bible with any regularity *not* because we're such busy people but rather because the Bible's vision of a transformed humanity would drastically threaten how we choose to live our lives. We cannot imagine a God who would dare to jump Moses and try to kill him in the wilderness. We prefer a tamer notion of God—flashbulbs and sweet smiles on the baptism day. But the Bible is clear: "It is a fearful thing to fall into the hands of the living God" (Heb. 10:31).

The book of Malachi is the last in the Old Testament. Not much is known about the book's namesake. In Hebrew, Malachi means, "My messenger." He preached about 450 years before the birth of Jesus and was mostly interested in faithful worship practices. Malachi was hard on priests (like me) and people who went through the motions of temple liturgical customs. But Malachi was mostly interested in helping people get an accurate understanding of God. God, according to Malachi, is no cuddly teddy bear in the sky. God is loving and forgiving. But God is also jealous and incredulous and shocked by human behavior. God is not all that understanding of other gods that creep into the lives of those who assemble for worship. God, in short, gets ticked from time to time. Malachi's job as divine messenger was to let Israel know these things. And for most of the book he does just that.

"This God that you delight in, this God about whom you sing dazzling hymns of praise, he's coming all right. Oh, yes. But who can endure that coming? You? Me? God is nobody's Santa Claus," Malachi seemed to say. "God has an agenda to change us. To purify us all with fire and cleanse this place with soap."[5] It's not a message many wanted to hear back then. Fire and soap. I daresay not many want to hear it now, which leads back to my premise about our Bible reading habits.

But Malachi's message, though rather harsh and direct, is just about the best news any of us could ever hear, for it reveals a God who loves us enough not to leave us as we are. "Just as I Am" we come to God, claims the old hymn. But God will not leave us that way. Is that good news or bad? Depends. I like to think it can be very good news.

Recently, during our church staff retreat at Lutheridge in the North Carolina mountains, we ran into a wild turkey at the camp that really wasn't all that wild. I nicknamed him Tom. This bird walked around loose but made absolutely no attempt to get away when approached.

In fact, one afternoon as we left camp Tom blocked our way at the exit and would not budge. We honked the horn. Tom stayed put. I figured residents of Lutheridge must be feeding Tom regularly and he was used to handouts—a sort of "poultry toll" assessed like some New Jersey Turnpike attendant. Tom stood firm with his gizzard out and would not move.

We finally put the car in reverse and exited camp in the wrong lane. But Tom wasn't done with us. He started chasing the car. I've never seen a turkey chase an automobile. As we turned onto Highway 25, I looked back through the rear window. Tom stopped at the camp boundary and returned to his avian post, waiting for the next car.

My comfortable life needs chasing down by the hungry. I got a close look at Tom's eyes through the window of our car. There was fire in them. "God is like a refiner's fire, like fuller's soap," says Malachi. God will not leave us as we are. We are loved too much to be left that way. Like Moses in the wilderness, God chases us down. God intends to kill us, to drown us in his watery grace, and to convert us more and more into his likeness.

Questions for Discussion

1. How might the church recover the idea of "dying with Christ" in the baptismal practices of your local congregation? Why is this important?

2. If you were the key planner, what might occur in the celebration of a baptismal anniversary for a child or adult?

3. Do you agree or disagree with the author's assumptions as to why people have stopped reading the Bible? Explain.

2

The Sanctification of Jesus: Change in the Son of God

Mama tries to clear up all confusion by saying that Christ is exactly what the Bible says He is. But what *does* the Bible say He is? On one page He's a Word, on the next a bridegroom, then He's a boy, then a scapegoat, then a thief in the night; read on and He's the messiah, then oops, He's a rabbi, and then a fraction—a third of a Trinity— then a fisherman, then a broken loaf of bread. I guess even God, when He's human, has trouble deciding just what He is.[1]

—David James Duncan, *The Brothers K*

The book of James is very concerned about the danger of showing partiality, making "distinctions" between groups of people. "Don't side with one type of person or exclude another based on their background," James basically says to the early church.[2] Good gospel advice, then or now.

Curiously, however, the Lord Jesus himself made such distinctions. He chose sides and showed partiality. Sure he did—at least at first. And I realize the last two words of that last sentence might trouble you: "At first."

Midway through the Gospel of Mark (7:24-31), Jesus decides to take a break in the coastal region of Tyre and Sidon. Our Lord has been a busy boy in the last few chapters—teaching, feeding thousands, healing the sick; my goodness, his cousin's head has been recently chopped off (Mark 6:17-29). It's been a stressful few days for Jesus. Consult a map in the back of your Bible and you'll soon discover that Tyre and

Sidon are about twelve miles apart, both perched on the balmy shores of the Mediterranean—placid, quiet little seaside towns where one could kick back, enjoy a nice beverage, and listen to seagulls calling and waves gently lapping at the sand, the lunar tidal cycles a perfect recipe for clearing the head. This story says that Jesus was staying at somebody's "house" (Mark 7:24), and I like to think this cottage was perched on a little hill with a nice view of the water. A porch, a few deck chairs—you get the picture.

The story also reports that Jesus "did not want anyone to know he was there." And I can certainly appreciate Jesus' feelings in this regard. I'm honored to be an ELCA pastor, of course, but there comes a time when one needs to get away and be anonymous for a while. I once wore a clerical collar at O'Hare airport in Chicago and made a private vow never to identify myself in such a way ever again when traveling. When a lovely young woman in seat 23A says, "I'm in sales. What do you do?", I must confess that it's sometimes tempting to lie. I understand perfectly our Lord's desire to be alone for a while. He did not want anyone to know he was there in that house by the sea.

But, of course, someone does learn he's in town. A woman barges onto the back porch, completely out of control, and "begs" Jesus to take action. She's in a puddle there at the feet of Jesus. Her adolescent daughter has "a demon." (And I think to myself: Isn't this normal? Don't *most* adolescent girls have demons? Can't this wait until Monday?) But this woman on the beach house porch is persistent. And at first you might conclude that Jesus puts her off because he's just worn out and needs a break. But that's not the issue here at all.

Jesus puts this woman off *not because he's tired*, but because she's an outsider. He basically says, "Look, lady, I feel for your situation and everything, but you're not one of us; you're not our kind. I've got a specific job description here that spells out exactly the sort of people I'm supposed to help and consort with, and I'm really sorry and every-thing, but you're just not on that list. Now would you please get off this porch?" Isn't that pretty much the gist of what he says? I won't even mention the name that Jesus calls this woman, but it's a rather rude reply no matter how one tries to explain it.

"Don't show partiality," says James in his epistle. "Don't make distinctions." But Jesus is doing both here by the sea. He helps this poor woman eventually but, as I said before, *not at first*. Now what do you make of this?

There have been various attempts to make sense of Jesus' behavior and soften the tenor of his words. One of the most compelling for me is that *even Jesus*, even our Lord, was on a "learning curve" when it came to keeping up with the Holy Spirit. To some that may sound rather blasphemous—to say that Jesus did not arrive in this world knowing everything and that he actually learned a thing or two as he went. But please remember that we say *two things* about Jesus in our creeds at the same time. Fully divine, yes, but also *fully human*. It's difficult to wrap our heads around this idea. It's hard for us to think of Jesus as someone who messed his pants as a baby, burped after meals as a kid, had a crush on the cute girl who sat across the room in school, and got teed off with his parents from time to time. But we say this very thing about Jesus in our creeds—he was Fully God, but also Fully Guy. Divine *and* human. In the Formula of Concord (1577), Lutherans believe Jesus "to be a bodily creature, to be flesh and blood . . . to move from one place to another, to suffer from hunger, thirst, cold, heat."[3]

If this is true, that even Jesus was on a learning curve when it came to understanding the will of God, is it not plausible that he could be rude to somebody whose name didn't seem to be included in his messianic job description? Does this seem like a stretch to you in making heads or tails of this story? If so, please stick with me just a bit longer. Come with me up the coast those twelve miles—up the coast to Sidon, still by the sea, right on the water.

Our story says that when Jesus left Tyre, he chose to head back towards the Sea of Galilee "by way of Sidon." Check again that map in the back of your Bible, and you'll soon discover that this is not the most direct route for Jesus to get back home. Sidon is *due north* of Tyre and the Sea of Galilee is *southeast*. Jesus is going well out of his way as he returns home from this little vacation junket. Is Jesus a little lost here? Or is there something going on with this odd geographical loop?

Somebody else puddles at the feet of Jesus there by the sea. It's another foreigner—a Greek guy who had struggled with hearing loss and a speech impediment all his life. Like the woman in Tyre, this man up the coast also was not on Jesus' original list; he was completely unrelated to anybody in Jesus' family of origin.

But watch what Jesus does. This gets my personal vote for the most unusual healing in the entire New Testament—a direct, personal affront to all of us who shower daily, trim our nose hairs regularly, and floss: Jesus puts his fingers into the deaf man's ears, apparently oblivious to the wax buildup of one of God's children who lived in a culture without indoor plumbing. Now, please note that the story says not a word about our Lord *washing* those waxy fingers. They go directly into or toward his mouth. Jesus then spits on those fingers that have been you-know-where. And then he touches the man's tangled tongue. With spit! And perhaps earwax. All of this occurred, don't forget, with a man who was every bit as much an outsider as that other foreign woman twelve miles down the beach.

Now stop a minute here and think about all this. Think about Jesus and the incredible theological *migration* (a seismic shift in evangelical outlook!) from exclusion to inclusion in these two stories. There is a huge sea-change here in the mission and ministry of Jesus. Right there along this twelve-mile stretch of water, Jesus has a change of heart. I don't know what you want to call it, but it comforts me that even our Lord and Savior was on something of a learning curve. In these two stories, Jesus dramatically moves from complete exclusion to rather shocking intimacy with outsiders. He begins by saying, "Go away," to one foreigner, and ends, literally, within spitting distance of another.

Long ago, in the early centuries of the church, ancient liturgies reveal that a bishop conducting a baptism would spit on his fingers and touch the mouth, ears, and eyes of the newly baptized. Perhaps the church had this rather odd healing of Jesus in mind. A baptized person, so touched by water and spit, would now see, hear, and speak in new and astounding ways.

"Be opened," said Jesus long ago. Who exactly was Jesus praying for here? I'm sure that Jesus was praying for the deaf man's ears. But you know, perhaps our Lord was also praying for *his own life*, now "opening" in ways he neither planned nor imagined.

This is not the only place in the New Testament where the early church seems to suggest that even Jesus grew and changed in the understanding of his mission and purpose. "Although he was a Son, he learned obedience through what he suffered" (Heb. 5:8). What a marvelously strange phrase this is. Jesus did not just pop out of Mary's womb pre-programmed, pliable, and perfect. In fact, the previous verse records that he learned obedience only through "loud cries and tears." In other words, he was not a robot, without free will and choice. He *learned* obedience. Earlier in the same book, the author claims that, "It was fitting that God, for whom and through whom all things exist, in bringing many children to glory, should make the pioneer of their salvation perfect through sufferings. For the one who sanctifies and those who are sanctified all have one Father" (Heb. 2:10-11). And, apparently, the crucified and risen sanctifier also once grew in his own understanding of sanctification. This is a simple statement on the face of it but an important one for Lutherans who contemplate their own sanctification and growth in the Spirit: *if Jesus was on a learning curve following his own baptism, how much more are his followers?* God is never through with any of us. "Even though our outer nature is wasting away, our inner nature is being renewed day by day" (2 Cor. 4:16).

I spend some time with the change in Jesus' own mission and ministry because there is no small amount of suspicion and mistrust among Lutherans when we speak of change and growth as a normal and expected part of the Christian life. This change can never be legislated or required in church life, but can we not expect and assume such? We will be *different* over time as a result of listening to God and living this story. If not, there is something terribly wrong.

"'Out of the believer's heart shall flow rivers of living water'" (John 7:38). This was a clear expectation of Jesus for those who named him Lord. After all, his own life was filled with surprising change and unforeseen detours as he became more and more open to the guidance and call of the Spirit.

Questions for Discussion

1. Why might it be troubling for some Christians to think of Jesus as a person who was "on a learning curve" in his own missional understanding?

2. Share an instance in your own faith life when you have struggled with or grown in your acceptance of "outsiders." What biblical or theological resources did you consider?

3

Will Work for Food: Effort and Discipline in the Sanctified Life

No one ever says, "If you want to be a great athlete, go vault eighteen feet, run the mile under four minutes," or "If you want to be a great musician, play the Beethoven violin concerto." Instead, we advise the young artist or athlete to enter a certain kind of overall life, one involving deep associations with qualified people as well as rigorously scheduled time, diet, and activity for the mind and body. But what would we tell someone who aspired to live well in general?[1]

—Dallas Willard

I should probably warn you from the beginning of this chapter that there are some things I'm about to say that will no doubt make card-carrying Lutherans rather nervous, even irritated. So have mercy on me.

There is a rather touching scene early in the Fourth Gospel where Jesus looks upon the crowds who are pursuing him (John 6:22-27) in what to me seems a somewhat sad, melancholy way. That may be an interpretive stretch since we cannot hear voice inflection in these old stories, but if we read it slowly, I think we can detect emotion and feelings in these words of Jesus.

His popularity is soaring, but Jesus is worried here about being misunderstood. After the feeding of the 5,000, the crowds go "looking for Jesus," hunting for the man. They pile into their boats and sail over to Capernaum. They find Jesus on the other side, but they have no idea how he could have possibly arrived there. *We* know how Jesus got there—his famous watery night walk across the open sea. But the crowds are certifiably baffled. "How in the dickens did you get over here?"

And this is where Jesus turns and looks at the crowds hunting for him. This is where he speaks to them with loving honesty, but also with some disappointment and, I think, sadness. He says, in so many words, "Let me tell you something, speaking the truth in love. All of you are looking for me not because you experienced something that drew you closer to God. You only want what I can do for you—the next whiz-bang picnic to fill your stomachs. You want another miracle from the traveling witch doctor. You really don't want *me* at all."

Isn't that what he basically said? And you know what? On most days, I must confess that I am in that crowd—wanting something from Jesus, but not *him* at all. I largely ask Jesus to fix this or that, bless my plans that I've already decided upon, and say "a little prayer" to let him know I'm still thinking of him from time to time. God help us, but perhaps that's true for many of us. We're interested in what Jesus can do for us, but it's a different thing to sit at his feet and learn how to live life from him. We think we can manage our lives just fine, throwing in a little Jesus when there's time, or if a jam arises.

And so Jesus looks at the crowds and says what I think is one of the most devastating and important things in any of the Gospels. He says, "Do not work for the food that perishes, but for the food that endures for eternal life, which the Son of Man will give you" (John 6:27).

I'm not going to spend much time on the first half of that statement, but I could. "Do not work for the food that perishes." It's fairly well documented that we spend inordinate amounts of time working for and acquiring "perishable" things. In a world of so many time-saving devices, it's curious that we claim to never *have* any time. Part of the problem is that we are drowning in our own stuff. I think we know this, even if we're not quite sure what to do about it.

My parents (now age eighty-two and seventy-eight, respectively) have started to sort through all their belongings and give away things, making sure keepsakes are earmarked for a particular person. It's a smart thing to recognize, at any age, that the possessions we've hauled around and worked so hard for are transient and perishable. "Do not work for the food that perishes," says Jesus. And yet I do. We do. A large part of my work and income funds perishable goods in exhausting, repeating, predictable ways. There's a sermon here, perhaps many sermons, but my focus here is on the second half of Jesus' statement to those crowds: "Work instead for the food that endures for eternal life."

It's the first little word in that part of Jesus' statement that usually trips up Lutherans—*work*. Very few people question the connection between gainful employment and the acquisition of material possessions. You work, you get paid, and you go and buy things. Indeed, our entire economy thrives on this idea—I've recently taken advantage of our statewide "no sales tax" weekend with the money my hard work has produced.

But try attaching the word *work* to our spiritual growth or growth in discipleship, and in Lutheran circles you are bound to hear some squawking. Why? "For we hold that a person is justified by faith apart from works prescribed by the law" (Rom. 3:28). Even though Jesus clearly uses the word *work* in the passage from John (which implies effort and some sort of spiritual striving), we have come to distrust this word because it doesn't seem, well, *Lutheran*. And so many, many Lutherans never get beyond a very common misunderstanding that Christianity is *only* about grace and the forgiveness of sins. "Jesus died for my sins." Believe that and you've got Christianity nailed (no pun intended).

It is true, of course, that Jesus died for our sins. But it is just silly and wrongheaded to believe that this describes *all* of Jesus' purpose. A popular post-communion prayer in *Lutheran Book of Worship* rightly affirms that Jesus is a "sacrifice for sin and a model of the godly life." But in truth, it's difficult for Lutherans (and many mainline Protestants) to talk honestly about the practical applications of the second half of that prayer. It is not only Jesus' death that makes us right with God but also his saving life. Bryan Stone, in the same work cited earlier, writes:

> The inbreaking of God's reign [in Jesus] both demanded and made possible an altered set of allegiances in which obedience to God relativizes one's family and national identities while calling into question customary patterns with regard to the status of women, children, the poor, and those otherwise ostracized or considered strange (tax collectors, prostitutes, lepers, Samaritans). These new patterns of kinship and social relation are not merely an *implication* of one's prior acceptance of salvation. Rather, they are precisely that which is offered *as* salvation.[2]

A rather large share of Jesus' teaching invites prospective disciples to become like him, to follow in his way, and to learn how to sin *less often*. This does not come naturally to us. I am largely a self-centered oaf obsessed with "food that perishes." It does not come naturally to me to behave otherwise. We are not born benevolent, kind, and sharing souls. Anyone who believes that hasn't been around babies and children for very long. We *learn* kindness and benevolence. And from whom do we learn these things? Well, from Jesus. Jesus is wonderfully patient in his intent to help us order our lives. He is infinitely willing to sit with us and teach us how to live life abundantly. His way of looking at and living life will see us through any tragedy, mishap, or challenge.

But here's the thing: *we must want that life*. Jesus does not wiggle his nose, and—*poof*—a mature Christian appears. Hear these words again: "Do not work for the food that perishes, but for the food that endures for eternal life, which the Son of Man will give you." Christ wants to give us this food. The sad thing is that we spend so much time acquiring, maintaining, protecting, and desiring the perishable food, and so little time working for the food that endures. We can never "earn" this enduring food. Christ wants to give it away. But we can *put forth the effort* so that we have free access to this grace.[3] This is what Jesus means by "working" for food that endures.

Our main problem in the world today is not economics or sectarian violence or drugs or any of those headline-grabbing things. In short, we mainly have a spiritual problem. We feed perishable food items to our spiritual hungers, and it doesn't work. It never has.

Christian Maturity

Paul's letter to the church in Ephesus makes several amazing claims and invitations concerning the Christian life. Please remember that Paul is the great crafter of our understanding of grace. Here are just a few things he says in a remarkable passage from Eph. 4:11-16, describing the sanctifying work of Christ through the church:

- We are called "to maturity, to the measure of the full stature of Christ" (v. 13). This implies that we will grow over time in our resemblance of Christ and our understanding of his will for us. Christ not only forgives us; *we are to become like him.*

- "We must no longer be children" (v. 14). Our understanding of Christ cannot remain stunted and immature over time. I always think of the theologian who said that even though Americans are extremely well-educated, many go through life with a "second-rate, second-grade Christian education."[4]

- "Speaking the truth in love [as Jesus does with his disciples in John], we must *grow up* in every way into him who is the head, into Christ" (v. 15, emphasis added). This is one of the main purposes of any congregation—not just to proclaim forgiveness (as important as that is), but to assist people of every age to grow in Christ.

On the back of our Sunday worship bulletin every week we print our congregation's vision statement—a variety of expectations and practices that we think will bring growth in Christ and growth to his church. In our monthly newsletter, readers find publicity for new small groups and classes meant to provide learning opportunities that will help foster theological maturity. One regular response to these groups and classes and expectations is to raise the red flag of legalism and ask, *"You mean I really have to do all this?"*

And my response is that, yes, *some* effort from the would-be disciple is required, if only to show up regularly. Jesus will do the rest in you, if given time and space to work. To be clear: spiritual disciplines have no saving effect in the life of a Christian. They simply give the Holy Spirit room to do its sanctifying work. What is certain is that we do not grow to Christian maturity through osmosis or luck. This will take some time (and effort) on your part.

Disciplines, Discipleship, and the Inner Life

One of the reasons that Jesus presses this question about our own effort is that he is clear (as we see elsewhere in the Gospels) about the real territory where spiritual change occurs. Have you ever noticed that when you're all alone during your waking hours, a constant conversation is going on deep inside you? The voice may be innocuous: "Gosh, I've got to get home to let the cat out." Or, it may be lewd and rather seductive: "My heavens, that Shakira is really hot!" Or, it may be vindictive: "Would all these idiots please get out of my way? I've got to be somewhere in fifteen minutes."

The voices comprise our "unfiltered" inner life, and we all have one—an odd assorted jumble of thoughts and feelings that no one else ever hears. A lot is going on in this inner life, if we pay close attention. What's really important to us resides there, known only to us. The inner life is the subconscious geography of imagination and creativity. Art, literature, and invention spring from this inner realm. Admittedly, some of what happens in this hidden life is fairly dark and sinister, and so we shield even our closest friends or spouse from the complicated spiritual terrain deep inside. But an important task of the Christian is letting Christ have room in this private space.

Of all the things that got Jesus into trouble and eventually killed, these words he spoke to the religious authorities and the crowds probably rank right up there near the top in contributing to his bloody demise: "Listen to me, all of you, and understand: there is *nothing* outside a person that by going in can defile, but the things that come out are what defile. . . . For it is from within, from the human heart, that evil intentions come" (Mark 7:14-15, 21, emphasis added). Those taking notes to amass a theological case against Jesus were surely scribbling furiously that day. This was a rather shocking thing to say out loud, for religious purity was clearly measured in Jesus' era according to *external* prohibition—what you did (or did not) eat, touch, drink, or celebrate, and whom you did (or did not) befriend, socialize with, or marry.

Take a look at the very interesting purity laws in Leviticus 11 and you will find a rather amusing list of dietary dos and don'ts. In verses 3-8 we learn, "You may not eat the camel, pig, or rock badger because these things *do not* chew the cud *and* have divided hoofs. This makes them unacceptable, unclean. Stay away from them if you know what's good for you." (That's my own loose translation, but it's close). We can all be thankful for these culinary prohibitions. More from Leviticus: "These you shall regard as detestable among the birds. They shall not be eaten; they are an abomination [I love that word, by the way]: the eagle, the vulture, the osprey, the buzzard. . . the ostrich, the nighthawk, the sea gull, the little owl, the cormorant, the great owl, the water hen, the desert owl, the carrion vulture, the stork, the heron of any kind, the hoopoe, and the bat" (Lev. 11:13 19). The Honeycutt family had a bat that somehow got into our kitchen last summer and I never once thought of eating it, so at least *here* I'm kosher with these purity laws.

There is something about religious expression that gravitates toward lists and prohibitions in order to shape morality and spiritual growth. And we know that this has never worked. "You may go anywhere in the garden and do whatever you'd like to do in the whole place except this one thing," said God long ago to those first two in Eden. "Do anything you want really but remember that you cannot eat the fruit of the tree of the knowledge of good and evil. Don't go anywhere near that tree. Don't touch the tree. Don't even think about it." And we know how that old story turns out. What was God thinking? The forbidden becomes overwhelmingly tempting.

And, of course, it's easy to read Leviticus and Genesis and laugh at these lists of religious no-no's and pretend we've graduated from them. No parent, to my knowledge, has ever worked out a perfect balance between prohibitive lists of rules for their children and the whole concept of freedom. We learn a lot about growing up in the school of consequence and hard knocks. As an adult, I still find myself saying both of these seemingly contradictory statements: (1) "It's a free country; I can do as I please," and (2) "There ought to be a law against that."

The preponderance of evidence from the dawn of time is that we have relied on external laws to try and shape inner morality. We have aggressive and just laws to protect civil rights in our country, but our nation today still struggles mightily with issues of race. Hate crimes in our country are on the increase. Visit the Web site of the Southern Poverty Law Center (which tracks these crimes) for some chilling examples.[5]

In short, external prohibition and list making cannot change the human heart. Jesus had this right: "For it is from within," he says, "from the human heart, that evil intentions come" (Mark 7:21). And then he goes on to list a messy stew of human woe that begins internally. Evil, Jesus seems to be saying, is rarely spontaneous. It is *hatched*, over time, deep inside of us, alongside that little voice I was talking about earlier that no one else hears. If this is true, wise churches and their pastors will spend a great deal of time on matters of the heart—teaching people how to read the Bible and find their story there; how to pray, meditate, and listen for the voice of God; how to learn to talk back to the many false voices that compete for our attention in this life.

The church traditionally has called these practices of prayer, worship, and Bible study by another name—disciplines. And, in a way, these disciplines can seem like another external list of rules: "Let's see, I've worshiped today—check that one off. Done my morning prayers—check. Read my Bible—check. *What a good little boy am I.*" But please look at these disciplines another way. These spiritual practices are not the things we do to get God to love us more than God already does; these are things we do that *give Jesus room to work* in our lives. These are things we do that allow Jesus to shape and change the inner terrain of the human heart. And if Jesus is right—that the human heart is the locus of all evil intention—should not we strive to give the man regular access there? This is what spiritual disciplines seek to do.

Let me share just a single personal example. I have not watched television regularly for almost twenty-five years. And that includes news broadcasts. I read about and try to keep up with the news, but I don't think I'm stretching it to say that we're absolutely saturated with sensational images and sound bites that we can do little about. It's not that I think television is inherently immoral. (And I do not stand in judgment of you if you happen to love television.) It's just that I came to realize my life and dreams and inner hopes were being shaped and formed by insipid and trite voices more than by the Bible and Jesus' vision of the kingdom of God. I'm not saying that a person has to give up television in order to be a faithful follower of Jesus. I am saying that it was instructive for me to examine closely what was truly shaping my imagination—my heart.

Again, the idea here is not to maintain a judgmental list of dos and don'ts. "Nothing going in can defile," says Jesus. And perhaps that includes television or anything else. But at some point we have to examine how much room we are truly giving to Jesus. This examination leads one to the gift of spiritual disciplines and helps us examine how much time we truly devote to the important task of allowing Jesus to rummage around and do business with our hearts.

I'll say it again. Inside each of us, beyond the din and clamor of daily life, is a voice that no one else hears; an unfiltered voice that reveals more about us than anyone truly knows. It is this voice that directs our actions and choices in this life in powerful and often destructive ways— the large unseen landscape of the inner life.

It's one of the most devastating things Jesus ever said to would-be disciples. "I know why you're looking for me. You're interested in what I can do for you. But you really don't want *me* at all. Do not work for the food that perishes, but for the food that endures for eternal life, which I will give you."

Jesus knows the real terrain and context for human change and transformation. It is the challenge of authentic discipleship to make meaningful and ample space for Jesus and the food he offers to heal the complicated territory of the human heart.

It's a good question for Lutherans. Are we willing to work for this food?

Questions for Discussion

1. Locate your church constitution and discover what actually defines a "member in good standing." Should we *require* certain behaviors and disciplines of church members? Why or why not?

2. Describe and discuss the process of assimilation and reception of new members in your congregation. Do you feel the process is adequate? Explain.

4

God's Power:
Listening for the Holy Spirit

Every second a million petitions wing past the ear of God. Let it be door number two. Get Janet through this. Make mom fall in love again, make the pain go away, make this key fit. If I fish this cove, plant this field, step into this darkness, give me the strength to see it through. Help my marriage, my sister, me. What will this fund be worth in thirteen days? In thirteen years? Will I be around in thirteen years?[1]

—Anthony Doerr, *About Grace*

Just before he died, Jesus climbed to the brow of a hill, probably the Mount of Olives, and looked out over the beautiful city of Jerusalem. As divided as the region is today, it is still a stunning place. As Jesus peered down on the city he must have felt waves of nostalgia, recalling the trips his family took there together or the time he got separated from his mom and dad and how his parents ran all over town, worried sick about their lost little boy. "Did you not know that I must be in my Father's house?" asked the precocious child. As he looked over the city just before his death, I like to think that Jesus remembered that question, peering down at the same temple, the same streets he walked as a child, maybe a favorite park or the storefront of a kind merchant who slipped him a piece of fruit or bite of candy. Jesus loved this city. It was in his heart.

The picture settles into his soul, frozen there in time like an old scene from a snow globe, captured under glass. Jerusalem was like many other towns in this regard, in its normality—the bustle of commerce, the rhythms of the day, prayers rising to God from the faithful, hope nurtured, lost, regained. Perhaps Jesus stood on the brow of that hill for a long time looking down on the city, maybe even knowing his own fate just a few days away. Height can give us perspective.

Do you think Jesus does this still? Does he look down on cities like mine from a high place? Does he see the bustle of commerce and politics at the state capital over on Gervais Street? The timeless flow of the Congaree River through the middle of town? Does he notice our lives, the kind words we share or those we wish we could take back? Does he look down on our churches and on the sadness and joy of our lives and see the full scope of them—past, present, and future? Does he watch us and pray over us from a high vantage point? I like to think this is true. "Likewise the Spirit helps us in our weakness; for we do not know how to pray as we ought, but that very Spirit intercedes with sighs too deep for words" (Rom. 8:26).

The church traditionally has referred to this scene as Jesus' "lament" over the city. You probably know that there is an entire book in the Bible—Lamentations—where a prophet cries and cries a river of tears over human foolishness and faithlessness. Laments are fairly common throughout the pages of scripture. I'm guessing that's probably the toughest thing about being a prophet—tears not only come easily; they flow all the time. I'm pretty sure I wouldn't want to be a prophet. I read through the news in "Section A" of the paper rather breezily, wincing at the world's woes, at the tragedies of my neighbors, but pretty much keeping my emotional distance. Prophets, conversely, have a hard time making it through "Section A" on any day of the week. Their prayer lives are laced with lament every morning, noon, and night.

As he looked down on the city that day, remembering no doubt the fond memories of the past, Jesus also *laments*. And though it doesn't say so explicitly, I'm guessing the man is crying as he offers these words, tears streaming down his face. His eyes are filled to overflowing as he says, "How often have I desired to gather your children together as a hen gathers her brood under her wings, and you were not willing" (Luke 13:34). These are among the saddest words ever uttered by Jesus.

This scene on this hill is a vitally important snapshot from the life of our Lord. These tears, this lament, this confession of his *inability to do just anything he wants* may present us with an image of Jesus that we're really not used to. When I was a little boy, I had a Bible filled with wonderful color plates from the life of Jesus. He fed 5,000 with a few scraps of bread and a couple fish. He walked across the windy sea like a swashbuckling sailor. He raised a little girl from the dead with a word and a touch. He swabbed a bit of spit in a deaf man's ears and the guy could hear again. I loved these old color plates because they revealed a *powerful* Jesus who could do anything. Anything he wanted or desired. I remember being so intrigued with that idea—this man who could change things, who could do it all.

But as he looks down on the city before his death, Jesus confesses, through tears, that there's something he cannot do. Jesus can do a lot of impressive things, but there's one thing beyond his control. He cannot *make us* love him. He cannot make us follow his ways and his teachings. He cannot control our lives without our assent. He certainly "desires" this. "Often," he says, often he has tried to gather his people like a mother hen. Jesus is an overachiever at a lot of things, but when it comes to overriding human will, even Jesus strikes out in that department.

We often hear God described as "all-powerful," and I think I know what people mean when they use the phrase. But consider the limits of God's power poured into the life of Jesus. He can do a lot of things, impressively, memorably, but here (by his own confession) is an arena of human traffic where the man is powerless. I've always liked C. S. Lewis's take on this, actually found on the lips of a demon in his classic book, *The Screwtape Letters*: "God cannot ravish," says this senior devil. "He can only woo."[2]

Sanctification is a process initiated by the Holy Spirit and grounded in the teachings of Jesus, drawing disciples more and more into his saving life. But God cannot override our wills in this matter. There can be no coercion. "If any *want* to become my followers, let them deny themselves and take up their cross and follow me" (Mark 8:34, emphasis added). Jesus is no arm-twister. We are not robots. God can only woo. We can successfully hide from God for years, even as an active member of a local congregation.

One of the questions eternally pondered by caring people (rightly so) is this one: *Why did God allow this to happen?* And if we think of God only as a series of color-plates from the Bible—parting seas, feeding multitudes, smiting tyrants—then the question may indeed lead us down some troubling theological paths, even to the ultimate loss of faith. If God is *all*-powerful, then would you please, dear God, pass a little of that power my way? Would you take care of this or that problem for me? Spread a little muscle over in a certain corner of the world?

But what if there are things that even God cannot pull off without our assent? What if human will is factored into the equation? What if God prefers rebellion over a flock of smiling, nodding, loving robots who swallow and assimilate God's teachings in pre-programmed religious bliss, something on the order of "The Stepford Disciples"? If it made for a better world, would you turn over your will in the matter—*removing all possibility of not settling under the inviting wings of Jesus*—in order to achieve peace? These are important questions as we ponder the nature and limits of sanctification.

And so Jesus stands on a hill. He looks over the city. Tears stream down his face. "How often," he says, "have I desired to gather you, but you were not willing. You would not assent. You desired another way, your own way." Jesus cannot *make* anyone love the way he loves. And he cannot protect us from the consequences of our rejection of such a way. "Your house is left to you," Jesus says (Luke 13:35). He will ultimately allow us to choose our own way if we insist upon such.

In the end, he can only hang there, looking down from another hill, arms spread wide like the wings of a mother hen, hoping that such a love will one day get the attention of a wayward world, of wayward people like me and you. God cannot coerce or shame us into Christian growth. He is powerful in many ways, but limited in his ability to make us love and follow. In some ways, sanctification is a divine "end-around" in our lives. The cross reveals an unexpected side of God who woos the world in paradox and restraint—"foolishness to those who are perishing, but to us who are being saved it is the power of God" (1 Cor. 1:18).

Saved in the Present Tense

Being saved. The verb tense is important here. On street corners in downtown America, on front porches after answering an urgent evangelical knock, in office spaces as we return the gaze of a well-meaning colleague, the question is consistently posed: "Are you saved?" The question seems to assume a once-and-for-all finality and safety for those who answer affirmatively.

The work of the Holy Spirit in the Bible is never final, static, or safe. Salvation is more of a process than a particular event that can be dated and described. We are "being saved." As an example of this truth, recall Jesus looking at Peter with love even as a servant girl brought Peter to denial for the third time (Luke 22:61). Even if Peter's growth as a disciple had ended right there around the fire, I daresay that Jesus would have loved and forgiven him. "Father, forgive them; for they do not know what they are doing" (Luke 23:34). But something happened to Peter fifty days later that no one could have predicted or scripted. The Holy Spirit swept behind closed doors (Acts 2:1-21) and the once-timid denier of Jesus preaches openly in the same streets that once hid his cowardice. God was not through with Peter. Salvation is a process for us all. God may be powerless to control my will if I'm inclined to rebel. But God does not leave me alone. God's grace is always close by in relentless pursuit. We are *being saved.* The tense is important.

"Surely goodness and mercy shall follow me all the days of my life" (Ps. 23:6). The Hebrew verb translated as "follow" in this familiar psalm is the same word used to describe Pharaoh as he "follows" the children of Israel in hot pursuit toward the Red Sea (Exod. 14:8). This is no gentle ambling as God follows us with goodness and mercy. God is tailing us and intends to catch us with gifts of goodness and mercy. God catches us at the sea (font) and drowns sin and pride in the water. God was not through with Peter, and God is not through with us. Salvation is always a process initiated, planned, and relentlessly pursued by the Holy Spirit.

In his *Large Catechism* (1529), Luther gave the title "Being Made Holy" to the third article of the Apostles' Creed:

This, then, is the article that must always remain in force. For creation is now behind us, and redemption has also taken place, but the Holy Spirit continues his work without ceasing until the Last Day, and for this purpose has appointed a community on earth, through which he speaks and does all his work. For he has not yet gathered together all of this Christian community, nor has he completed the granting of forgiveness. Therefore we believe in him who daily brings us into this community through the Word, and imparts, increases, and strengthens faith through the same Word and the forgiveness of sins.[3]

Trusting the Spirit's Directional Nudges

Examples of this restless "work without ceasing," this pursuit of the Spirit in the process of salvation (and respect of our human freedom in the matter), are found throughout the Bible. I want to examine one provocative story of the Spirit's work from the book of Acts, the conversion of Lydia (Acts 16:6-15). But first, a couple of reassuring caveats for Lutherans who normally are shy about such things.

Occasionally, I meet people who make me rather nervous about their utter and complete certainty that God is directing every single moment of every single day for the six billion (or so) people on the planet, if only we would each listen hard enough for God's voice. The next hours for such a person are always mapped out with exacting divine precision, a direct pipeline to the Almighty that instructs them to go here or there and refrain from doing this or that. A cynical inner voice wonders if God instructed them to brush their teeth at precisely 6:17 a.m. that morning or take out the trash at 9:43 p.m. before retiring. For someone who takes seriously the gift and responsibility of human freedom *and* the urgent work of the Holy Spirit, such scheduled certainty feels all too mechanical for my Lutheran sensibilities, almost like a puppet on a string. In some ways this theological position would make things easier, much easier in fact but, again, I must confess to a disdain for the life of robotic Pinocchio before he was a real boy.

Having said that, I also get nervous around people of faith who want to remove God altogether from the daily details of a given twenty-four-hour period of time. Such people love and respect God as a powerful deity who created the world and set "natural law" in motion long ago and then, well, stepped back without interfering at all in human affairs. Theologians call this "deism." Thomas Jefferson (among several of our founding fathers) was a deist. I have to admit that such a theological position *does* solve a lot of problems ranging from tsunamis in the Indian Ocean to genocide in Darfur to a deranged shooter at Virginia Tech. There is a siren theological appeal to thinking that God originally "wound up" the world like a clock and then stepped back to see what humans would do with it, factoring in a tragedy here or there because we happened to get in the way of the "natural order" of things now set inexorably in motion. Ultimately, this position also feels rather depressing and a breath away from giving up God entirely.

The conversion of Lydia is a good test case for these reflections as we ponder the sanctifying work of the Holy Spirit in Acts. It all seems *so clear* for those first believers. Paul, Timothy, and Silas are on a little missionary junket. Here's their testimony as I understand it: "You know, we wanted to go over into Asia, but the Holy Spirit wouldn't let us go there—Asia was off-limits, forbidden. *Verboten.* And so then we got our maps and thought maybe Bithynia on the northern coast was our next destination. We tried to go there, but the Spirit of Jesus said no." I get this image of Jesus standing at the Bithynian border with a helmet, badge, flashing light, and stop sign. (I often wish Jesus would appear to me this way when I'm about to do something dunder-headed. "No, Frank, you cannot go there. Sorry, old boy.")

And then finally Paul has a dream or a night vision—take your pick. A desperate Macedonian needs help. "Come over here and help us," says the Macedonian. I'm not sure how Paul recognized this guy *as* a Macedonian since he's never been to Macedonia (or anywhere near this far from home) in his entire life, but let's not quibble over these details. As one Bible paraphrase puts it: "The dream gave Paul his map."[4]

Now see, let's stop right here a moment. We're Lutherans, okay? Lutherans are fairly suspicious about this sort of testimony. We don't change course easily or quickly. Ten years from now we'll still be talking about what we miss in the green book. We don't trust easy fixes or faith widgets or snazzy theological gizmos or people swept away in the Spirit. We prefer a church with a *nailed-down* theology (think about that image) and few surprises. I'll just admit this out loud: *The book of Acts makes Lutherans nervous.* The Holy Spirit lands on shy people in fire and wind (Acts 2). The Holy Spirit directs a disciple to go to the desert and board a coach next to a sexually suspicious guy from Timbuktu (Acts 8). The Holy Spirit sends dreams to people—a bed sheet coming out of heaven, for crying out loud—directing us to go here and there, befriending people who are not our kind (Acts 10). The Holy Spirit calls a cad like Saul ("the man who made havoc") and transforms the guy into somebody who won't shut up about Jesus, who actually listens to voices in the night (Acts 9).

Please. My life isn't like this. My life is rather mundane and pedestrian compared to these characters in Acts. And you know what? If truth were told, I *don't want* the kind of life described here. I don't want it. I want to be free. Doesn't God (as we've noted above) respect my freedom to choose? Doesn't God allow me to figure out what I want to do with next Wednesday or the next few months and years in my life? I'll say it again: The book of Acts makes me nervous. For heaven's sake, I'm a Lutheran, after all.

And yet . . . and yet I can look back on my life and see certain twists and turns in it that make me think I really wasn't so free after all. Lutherans have a fairly safe word when we finally get around to thinking this way. We call it *discernment*. We look back and we "discern" the Spirit's presence in this or that event. I'm a big fan of discernment, don't get me wrong, but in Acts the Spirit doesn't wait around until those people find the time to do such a thing. But maybe discernment is a start.

I look back on my life in astonishment and start to consider how certain decisions and certain meetings of certain people, even a seemingly random conversation, led me this place, then that one, and now here. Now think with me a moment. If *any of us* had done just one or two things a little differently, we would be altogether different people living an altogether different life.

Thirty years ago, if I had gone to Auburn instead of Clemson, as originally planned, I never would have met two Lutheran pastors who influenced me greatly (seminary was not even on my radar screen at the time; neither was church, for that matter). I never would have worked at a certain summer camp or met someone named Cindy with whom I would have three altogether unique children. Had I gone to Auburn instead of Clemson, I would be a vastly different person, maybe working as an engineer for some company in Idaho. If you want to go further back than that, I can tell you that my parents met on a blind date that was scheduled at the last minute. They were working in different towns at the time. If not for that date and their subsequent courtship, I wouldn't even *be*. I daresay we can all do this sort of odd reconstructive history that reveals moments adding up to something more than random chance.

"And so we tried to go to Asia, but the Spirit forbade us. Bithynia looked appealing, but the Lord said no. I finally had this dream that ultimately led me to this woman beside a river on the outskirts of Philippi on the Sabbath day. Her name was Lydia. She had her own company selling purple cloth. Her heart was opened to the Lord." A church started on the banks of that river with a woman who was most likely the first convert to Christianity in Europe. We hear more about that congregation in Paul's letter to the Philippians.

Now I realize that when we hear folks talk this way—arranging their lives by listening to dreams, voices, and gusts of wind—it all seems rather hokey and contrived. But even as Paul was led oddly to this woman of purple whose heart was opened to the Lord by that river, so we too can reconstruct how (and maybe why) we've come to this moment in time.

A "purple heart" is usually given to those who are wounded in battle. As with Lydia, the woman of purple, our hearts have been found by God (sometimes even as we battle him) for a reason. We bring our wounds and joys into a community where God calls us to share life together. We call this "church." Luther calls this "being made holy." Older versions of the catechism call this "sanctification."

And so I wonder. What if we have been led to this point in our lives to do something utterly monumental and vitally important? What if all those chance bends and turns in your life's road really were not luck at all? What if we are poised together at the edge of the sea, the font of the Lord, and God is giving us dreams to answer? Voices to attend to?

God is speaking to us, calling us. Paul was certainly free to say no to the Spirit's prodding that led him to Philippi. Peter was free to remain ashamed and embarrassed by his Holy Week denials. This is true for any of us. God cannot ravish; God can only woo. But let me tell you: it's a relentless and insistent wooing.

Questions for Discussion

1. How would you describe to a new Christian the limits and nature of Jesus' "power"?

2. Discuss the difference between "being saved" and salvation in the past tense.

3. Share a key detail or two from your past without which your life would be completely different. Can you discern the Spirit's presence in these moments?

5

Catechesis: The Sanctifying Power of Teaching

Just then there was in their synagogue a man with an unclean spirit.
—Mark 1:23

If, according to Luther, church is the communal context for the process of sanctification, then it behooves us to pause and examine the depth and purposes of faithful catechesis offered in such a setting.

Let's say we're all gathered one morning in our Sunday best, filing forward for the bread and wine, and a wild, disheveled-looking person runs down the center aisle, shouting something unintelligible. He knocks over a few children in his rowdy wake, throws back a wild head of hair, and yells something about Jesus. Eyes roll back in his skull, and with a thud, he hits the floor in convulsions—spit all over the new carpet. It happens so quickly, no one has time to think about finding an exit.

An odd, other-worldly voice eerily inquires into the air, *"What have you to do with us, Jesus?"* Paramedics finally arrive. A single injection quiets the crazy voice. He seems to walk out quietly and even shakes the hand of an usher on the way to the ambulance. Perhaps we continue with the service, needing bread and wine that morning more than we thought. Maybe we say a quick prayer for the man. But here's a reaction I'd guess nobody would ever offer. I suspect no one in the assembly would rise and say, "Glory be! A new teaching!" (Mark 1:27).

A new teaching? Is that what those people said that morning?

The Gospels assume the palpable reality of personified evil in the ministry of Jesus. Our Lord serves as exorcist with some frequency. It's interesting in Mark's Gospel that the demons are the ones who know Jesus from the story's opening curtain, while the disciples, the consummate insiders, remain unusually obtuse from start to finish. Ponder that.

Most modern people (despite the occasional popularity of movies such as the recent film, *The Exorcism of Emily Rose*) do not actually believe in the demonic, relegating such paranormal expression to psychological abnormality. I'm certainly no expert on demons, remaining rather agnostic about their existence—specific and nameable evil, yes; an honest-to-goodness talking demon, well, I'm not sure. But I do want to point out a couple things from Mark's story that Christians concerned with adult conversion and issues of sanctification might want to reflect upon with some seriousness.

First, I find it very telling that Jesus' early encounter with evil did not happen in some shadowy, out-of-the-way, ominous location with dark clouds and a brewing wind. He's not on his way to Mordor and Mount Doom, for example, the famous locus of evil in Tolkien's *Lord of the Rings* trilogy. Nor is he confronting evil in some obviously forbidden locale such as a brothel, crack house, or gambling casino.

Jesus is standing *in a place of worship*, a synagogue, on the Sabbath. And even though there are obvious differences in the two places, let's just say he was standing in church one Sunday when evil emerged. Only twenty verses into this earliest Gospel, Jesus takes on evil in a rather surprising context.

I recall a baptism several years ago where I invited the children forward to get a better view of the sacrament. My son Lukas, four at the time, was among the children who came up to the font. When we came to the "renunciation" part of the baptismal liturgy—"Do you renounce all the forces of evil, the devil, and all his empty promises?"—with his own devilish grin, my son looked up at his pastor/father and replied, "No!" This brought down the house, of course, but I think back on that answer and confess my own hesitancy to renounce all that glitters and seduces, all that blocks and derails my own growth in discipleship. I remember approaching my systematic theology professor, Dr. Michael Root, in seminary and asking with some skepticism, "Do I *really* have to say that old line about the devil and his empty promises?" I'll never forget his response. Dr. Root patiently smiled at me and said, "Spend twenty years in parish ministry and come back and ask me that question again." He was right. The church is not a special haven from the demonic.

But here's the thing that really gets me from this old story in Mark. It's easy to focus on the healing itself—the convulsive tongue now silent; the loud voices quieted; the drama and eeriness of exorcism. "Could that have really happened?" our modern minds wish to know. Please notice exactly *how* this healing happens. Jesus isn't waving a magic wand or wiggling his divine nose. What exactly is Jesus doing in that synagogue on that particular Sabbath day? Well, our Lord is teaching. He's teaching Sabbath school. In fact, it's precisely the *teaching* of Jesus that seems to flush out the demons in the first place. Evil doesn't greet Jesus at the door, but only *after* the kingdom lessons begin. "Just then" (v. 23) the demoniac appears, grovels around on the floor, and knocks over the dry-erase board that Jesus was using that morning to illustrate his theological point.

This scene should remind any teacher what is at stake in preparing and delivering lesson plans or sermons in the local congregation. "Hey, it's just Sunday school for heaven's sake; it's just worship." Beware of that mentality. Very often, we want a tame, innocuous Jesus who will forgive whatever behavior seems right to us at the time, a man who pets sheep and dangles children on the knee, a sweetly domesticated Jesus, delivered in manageable doses, who never rocks the boat. I frankly desire a version of Jesus who will teach me as long as he can be wedged into whatever is already going on in my life.

The demons are the ones who really recognize what's at stake here, and they start their nervous chatter. "What have you to do with us, Jesus of Nazareth?" And see, that's our question, too, if we're honest, deep down. *What have you to do with me, Jesus?*

Please don't forget this detail: all this happened in church, not in some dark alley—a reminder that more may be at stake on Sunday mornings than we ever imagined. Jesus will be resisted, even in church settings, perhaps especially there. He will liberate some and anger others with his teaching. If we really believed that *teaching* actually drives out evil spirits in our lives, would there be more or fewer people in the classes we offer? I go back and forth on that one. Change is hard work. We are often content to remain the same because it's worked so well for so long.

I doubt you've ever heard of Marian Conrad, Margaret Byassee, or John Foster. How about Gene Copenhaver, Ron Luckey, or Joe Warner? Well, you would have been blessed to know them. In church and school settings, they were among the best teachers I ever had. They affirmed me in the formative years of my cognitive and faith development. And I know they loved me, which was important. But they also taught me uncomfortable lessons about life that I would have never learned on my own, never would have chosen had the choice been entirely up to me. They dared to tread among demons. Some of them I cursed at the time, because they expected a lot. They were master teachers. And I never heard audible demonic voices in class or during a particular sermon or Sunday school lesson. But their words still haunt me in their truth and power. Teaching and faithful catechesis can have that sanctifying effect on us.

Here early in the twenty-first century, we tend to assign most severe problems to the realm of psychology (and thank God for the insights of that particular field). But sometimes our problems are not psychological at all. We simply flounder at times from lack of insight, even laziness, in learning. In the novel, *The Good Priest's Son*, an aging Episcopal rector, Tasker Kincaid, listens to a confession concerning chronic and unhealthy lust from his son, Mabry, whose recent divorce was fueled by an affair. Father Kincaid listens closely in his uncomfortable dual role as dad and confessor, and then says: "…my observation after sixty years of close sin-watching is that pure *laziness* tops the list. Most people persist in all the other wrongs just because they're too satisfied with lying motionless on their bed or couch—or the couch in their *mind*—to stand up and change."[1]

In the early church, an entire Gospel was written specifically for a young adult convert, so that he might "know the truth concerning the things about which you have been instructed" (Luke 1:4). That last word comes from the Greek verb, *catecheo*. The early church knew precisely what was at stake in patient instruction and quality catechesis. Jesus flushed out and confronted evil very early in his ministry with a rather surprising mechanism: his teaching. If people do not wish to change, if folks have no intention of looking at life in a new way, then by all means the church should counsel curious seekers to stay away from the teachings of Jesus. For the man apparently means to do business with the demons in the lives of people like us who thought we left all that behind upon entering a mature adulthood.

The question on the lips of the demons is also our question. *What have you to do with us, Jesus of Nazareth?* Indeed, what have you to do with me?

Living in the Ellipsis
While Mark begins his Gospel in an unusual way, inviting the church to consider the importance of teaching in the process of adult conversion, the ending to Mark's Gospel (16:1-8) also encourages any congregation passionate about sanctification (growth in discipleship and holiness) to reflect critically upon the particular processes that must be in place to form disciples capable of living the way of the cross.

On most Sunday mornings across our nation there are more than a few people in our church pews who are not totally convinced that Jesus rose from the dead. *Something* surely happened early one Sunday morning close to 2,000 years ago, to be sure. That much cannot be denied even by a certified skeptic. But of all the people assembled Sunday in and out, there's more than a handful (members and non-members alike) who have a couple questions about how a completely dead guy gets up and begins to walk around. A working assumption: there is a lot more doubt in the pews than many are willing to admit. That includes pastors, of course. Heck, it includes me.

Some people, of course, are absolutely sure of Easter and the surrounding details; the questions settled long ago. And others don't believe a word of it and maybe never will. My friend Andy, who lives on fifty acres in Maine, two miles from the nearest power line, has been a faithful letter-writing companion for almost thirty years. He once wrote that if he ever did meet God on the road one fine day, he'd "chase him down with a pitchfork." My friend represents those who think the sacraments are "as silly as a séance."[2]

But there are others (perhaps attempting to live out the ramifications of Easter, that outlandish gift) who have lots of questions—not quite ready to pin their whole lives on such a possibility, but open nonetheless. Part of the intent of this book is to grapple with an important question: What does the church *do* with such people? What is our theology of sanctification that informs parish initiation rites and conversion processes which give the Holy Spirit room to shape and form new lives?

In three of the Gospels—Matthew, Luke, and John—Jesus is crucified on a Friday and then on Sunday he's up and about and, well, *viewable*. One time he's mistaken for the gardener (John 20:15). Another time he hikes (incognito) along a road several miles with two guys who don't recognize him until broken bread opens their eyes (Luke 24:30-31). And still another time Jesus is frying fish on the beach and calls the disciples out of their boats to a big breakfast (John 21:12). I love these stories. Jesus, once dead, now walks, talks, and moves around—clear, happy endings as Jesus gives specific directions to his followers who, in some accounts, watch slack-jawed as their Lord ascends into heaven (Acts 1:11).

But the Easter story from Mark's Gospel records none of these sightings of Jesus. Please note: in Mark's Gospel, the resurrected Jesus *never once appears* (which is rather comforting, if you think about it, for a modern congregation of people who can no longer rely on such physical viewings). The most reliable versions of this Gospel end at verse 8: "[The women] said nothing to anyone, for they were afraid." The early church was clearly uncomfortable with this conclusion and tried to fashion another ending or two, tacking them on to the original. (A theological sidebar: this is where we get the rather strange business about snake-handling and drinking strychnine without harm). But for the lion's share of scholars of this Gospel, Mark ends rather abruptly. It's almost like ending a story with an ellipsis.

So, for the record, careful readers of Mark's account will receive nothing more than this: an empty tomb, a young man offering vague instructions, and three women filled with pure and holy terror—end of story. It's hardly the "Hallelujah Chorus." We want more, but there is no more. The credits roll, the curtain falls, and Mark's version of the Easter saga is done. So much for happy endings tied up with a neat moral bow.

These early Christians did not depend on actual Easter *sightings* of Jesus at all. This early community for whom Mark wrote did not define "resurrection" as actually viewing a once-dead man. So here I want to return to my previous hunch: there are quite a few people in our congregations each Sunday morning who are *open* to Jesus, but have no idea how a completely dead guy gets up and walks around. Now don't get me wrong. I'm perfectly comfortable with a once-dead Jesus walking around. In fact, I believe such things and say so in the creeds regularly. But here's the curious thing: *for Mark*, these visual sightings of Jesus did not an Easter make. What, then, was Easter for Mark?

The women in this story intrigue me. You've got to give them credit because the men are nowhere to be found—not a single guy out this early. But it's the progression of emotion from these women that really grabs my attention. On the way to the tomb, they seem fearless and only concerned with the weight of the stone. Even upon encountering the young man in the white robe, they are only "alarmed" (16:5). Alarm is different from fear. They are filled with terror and say nothing to nobody and run for the hills *only* when they hear the words of this young man. Remember those words? "He is not here," says the young man. "He is going ahead of you to Galilee; there you will see him, just as he told you," (Mark 16:6-7). And off the gals go, "for they were afraid." End of story.

For me, that little geographical hint is the whole key to Mark's Easter. "He's going ahead of you to Galilee." And then it hits them. Galilee is the very place where Jesus originally called those first fishermen and invited them to follow. Galilee is where the demons emerged in worship that Sabbath day. In other words, the women are told that they will find Jesus, *the resurrected Jesus*, exactly where the sick, poor, leprous, despised, and possessed happen to live. *That's* Galilee—then and now.

"You really want to see Jesus?" the young man seems to ask. "Well, you just missed him. He's not here. *You're looking in the wrong place.* You'll find him from now on in the Galilee of a thousand different towns, wherever people are thirsty for the good news." The story has come full circle; it's starting over again—and now we're invited to join the narrative, where the cross awaits all who've been baptized. There *is* a way to experience resurrection in this Gospel. Mark paints the choice clearly. We can follow, or we can run. There are a thousand ways to run.

Faithful catechesis matters greatly as we participate in the Holy Spirit's plan to change and convert the church. Pastors and other congregational leaders are called to name creatively in class settings the specific ways our people are bound, and how this binding prevents faithful following to the cross and beyond. "One little word subdues him," claims Luther of the devil in his famous hymn. "The word of God is living and active, sharper than any two-edged sword, piercing until it divides soul from spirit, joints from marrow; it is able to judge the thoughts and intentions of the heart" (Heb. 4:12). Something like an exorcism occurs in the process of faithful teaching of God's word. "For our struggle is not against enemies of blood and flesh, but against the rulers, against the authorities, against the cosmic powers of this present darkness, against the spiritual forces of evil in the heavenly places" (Eph. 6:12).

Ron Allen, well-known professor of preaching, writes how sermons can have the effect of naming and casting out demons in the church. I invite you to use the words *teacher* and *teaching* where he refers to *preacher* and *preaching*:

> Rather than making the people in the pews the enemy, the preacher
> focuses critique on the powers of death that hold people captive. The
> preacher does not stand against the congregation, but rather stands
> with them as one who also struggles with complicity in the face of
> the powers; all stand together in need of redemption through the
> Word. The preacher does not "beat up on people" or load them with
> guilt, but rather seeks to set them free, possibly even tapping into

their longing for release. Preaching thus moves beyond simplistically condemning or challenging individuals, and moves toward naming and confronting the powers that hold people captive.[3]

The first chapter of Mark's Gospel contains an exorcism brought on by faithful teaching. And the last chapter ends in ambiguity, invitingly unclear whether disciples of Jesus have the theological wherewithal to follow him in a world such as ours. The curtain falls on Mark's story. Or does it? Jesus has told us where we can find him. Remember: this story does not end with a period. It ends with an ellipsis—"to be continued" in your life and mine.

Living squarely in the midst of this ellipsis, the church is fortified, formed, and given courage to follow Jesus by the sanctifying work of the Holy Spirit moving in and through the community's teaching ministry.

Questions for Discussion

1. Share your own understanding of the devil and the demonic. Reflect upon the importance of "renunciation" in the baptismal liturgy.

2. Describe a favorite teacher from your past. What made the person's teaching effective? How was the teacher an agent in "casting out demons"?

3. What about learning ministry is exciting in your congregation? What needs to change?

6

Sanctification, Resurrection of the Body, and the Call of God

Look at my hands and my feet; see that it is I myself. Touch me and
see; for a ghost does not have flesh and bones as you see that I have.
—Luke 24:39

The explanation of the third article of the Apostles' Creed, to which
Luther affixes the title "On Being Made Holy" in the *Small Catechism*,
includes, of course, the famous line, "I believe in the resurrection of the
body." To believe in such a physical resurrection, according to Brother
Martin, contributes mightily to a Lutheran theology of sanctification and the holiness of Christ's church *in this life* as well as the next.
Unfortunately, Luther does not engage in his classic question and
answer formula in either catechism when describing the value of such
bodily belief. Lutheran theologian David Yeago suggests: "It is probably a bad habit among Lutherans always to address such issues [of
sanctification] by interpreting the reformers rather than turning to
Holy Scripture."[1] With that in mind, I turn to three Bible stories that
shed some light on this part of the creed—one resurrection narrative
from Luke and two "call" stories from Isaiah the prophet and Peter the
erstwhile fisherman.

The Raising of Flesh and Bones[2]
My wife and I traveled recently to Ocracoke Island on the Outer
Banks of North Carolina, returning to the site of our honeymoon, to
celebrate our twenty-fifth wedding anniversary. The island is home to

a variety of ghost stories about pirates, shipwrecks, and other lost souls. Many claim that Blackbeard himself still prowls the coves and alleys of Ocracoke.

Travel down the coast several hundred miles to Pawley's Island and you might find the famous "Grey Man," a misty apparition who appears before storms to warn residents of approaching bad weather. My own city is said to have its share of specters and spooks. Ghost tours are held regularly after dark, for a small fee, on the South Carolina State House grounds in Columbia.

We are fascinated with the shadowy netherworld between earth and heaven—deceased folk who roam the earth trying to complete unfinished business. One of the most popular movies of the last twenty years is *The Sixth Sense*, a tale about a precocious little boy who notices tormented souls all around him. If you've seen the movie, you'll never forget the boy's confession to his counselor—"I see dead people." The film was popular because it dealt cleverly with a question we all ask but cannot answer with any certainty: "What happens to people just after they die?" Fiction, cinema, and television all deal with this question on a fairly regular basis. I remain rather agnostic about the presence of ghosts, but parishioners have told me over the years of their certainty in seeing one or more. My mother still swears she saw a ghost years ago in the home of a childhood friend.

Even the Bible indulges in these questions. Consider the strange story in 1 Sam. 28:3-19, where King Saul, obsessed with the growing popularity of David, consults the Witch of Endor. She practiced the art of necromancy, which was forbidden in Israel by Saul himself. But these were desperate times for the paranoid king, so Saul (in disguise) knocks on the medium's door in the middle of the night. They conduct a rather eerie séance and conjure Saul's mentor, Samuel, who is not pleased about being roused from the land of the dead. "Why have you disturbed me by bringing me up?" asks Samuel.

You also might recall that the disciples, upon viewing Jesus walk toward them across the sea in "the fourth watch" of the night, are fairly sure they are seeing a spook (Matt. 14:22-27). In most every religion and culture, people have wondered about the existence of ghosts.

It's interesting that Jesus takes special pains in an Easter story from Luke's Gospel (Luke 24:36-43) to show the disciples that he's no Casper the Friendly. "Why are you frightened?" he wants to know. "Touch me. Let your fingers do the walking. I'm no ghost, no shadowy apparition. Do ghosts have flesh and bones? Anybody have any broiled sea bass handy? Serve me up a piece and I'll prove it." Notice: even in resurrection, the wounds of Jesus are visible.

I remember a church softball game several years ago where I slid into second base wearing shorts—dumb move, lots of blood. After I washed the wound and affixed a bandage, a little boy walked up to me and said something I couldn't quite make out at first. I leaned down to listen. He whispered, "Can I touch your boo-boo?" I recall how he reached out with his little index finger to touch the bandage. Even at a young age, we are moved by the wounds of others and have a need to touch one another and bring healing to hurt places.

After his resurrection, Jesus enters *another* life with evidence of his *past* life. Easter transforms our wounds, but never pretends they did not exist. Sometimes, a Christian obsession with heaven tends to negate what we've experienced (both the good and bad) on this earth. This Easter scene with Jesus and his disciples suggests the two realms are always and forever connected. "Look, here are my wounds," says Jesus. "Touch them and see that it's really me." The real me and you, I'm convinced, will experience that future Easter much the same way. Our wounds will be overcome and transformed, but God will not pretend they never happened. If that were true, it would mean someone *other than me*, the real me, is being resurrected.

This is why Jesus spends some time parting ways with ghost-hood in this story; parting ways with an afterlife that's only some ephemeral everlasting where wispy spirits bounce on a beach in eternal, blissful rapture. "I believe in the resurrection of *the body*," we say in the creed. And although I cannot pretend to know what that body will look like, or when precisely it will be resurrected, our centuries-old understanding of this creedal claim is that Easter, the other side of the grave, involves physicality, matter, touch—*bodies* and their resurrected, transformed shape.

The old idea that the soul or spirit, the supposedly "good" part of a person, somehow splits off from the discarded shell of the body and floats away to heaven is not a Christian idea at all. It's a very old Greek idea known as the "immortality of the soul." The Apostles' Creed refutes this ancient reasoning. "I believe in the resurrection of the body" is an affirmation of what Jesus was affirming in that room as he ate that meal of fish and chips. "Do ghosts have flesh and bones?" he asks. "Do ghosts eat sea bass?"

Jesus' Easter appearance as someone with a body (rather than someone who appears as a wispy spirit) has all sorts of important theological implications for this life and a Lutheran theology of sanctification. Jesus is affirming the positive physicality of *this world*. We sometimes fall into the bad habit of believing it's the "spiritual" that is somehow a higher plane, the rarefied air of having arrived as a "real" Christian, which will ultimately come to fruition in the next life; a life completely disconnected from this one. And so we lapse into the false conviction that this earth and its many physical urgings are bad. The really pure self, we are led to believe, is the exalted "spiritual self." With these false assumptions, it's not such a huge jump to see the entire physical world as temporary, expendable, discardable—a holding tank until the really good world comes along. I am convinced that our national obsession with the *Left Behind* series is fueled by the non-biblical convictions that this earth (pronounced "good" by the creator numerous times in Genesis 1) is summarily "bad." Only infidels are "left behind" in such a place. This striving for a more pure and removed spiritual existence is an old heresy known as Gnosticism.

I've heard Christians say that we really don't need to get all that upset about the state of the environment because we're going to a better place where we won't have to worry about such tiring topics as global warming and the greenhouse effect. The Bible refuses to play along with this false dichotomy. Revelation, for example, claims that instead of "going" to heaven, *heaven is coming towards us* (Rev. 21:1-4). Catherine of Siena, a fourteenth-century mystic, echoed this idea when she wrote: "All the way to heaven is heaven." Jesus was concerned with resurrecting and affirming the body; blessing and giving thanks for the physical. "The kingdom of God is like this," he would say, holding up a mustard seed, pointing to ravens, calling our attention to lilies, and asking for fish at an Easter meal.

Several years ago I drove by a nursing home in rural southwest Virginia. Out behind the facility, I noticed about fifty wheelchairs, all in a crazy, mixed-up pile. I figured it must have been time for a mass washing, a spring bath with a big garden hose. But for me, the image of all those wheelchairs in a big stack is also an Easter preview. Like Jesus, we will be transformed. Our bodies will be changed. But this will not negate our earthly experiences, our wounds in this life, as if they never happened. Heaven will always have much to do with earth. According to this old Easter story from Luke, we will not be disembodied spirits floating around.

Don't ask me how (or when) this resurrection happens. But I will tell you, it's a great and wonderful promise that has everything to do with how we live this life. For Jesus, *matter* matters. "A ghost does not have flesh and bones as you see that I have." The resurrected Jesus was no ghost. He took special pains to show the disciples that he had a body. Easter, according to this old story, is about the raising of flesh and bones—not spooks—in this life (conversion) and in the next (fulfillment).

Isaiah and Peter: The Transformation of Daily Work

I remember a conference I once attended with Rollie Martensen, who teaches at Luther Seminary in Minnesota. Rollie told a story of when he was a young pastor living in Southern California near the Mexican border. One summer morning, just as he was leaving the house to play tennis, the phone rang. It was the local supermarket. The church had an arrangement with the store to pick up hamburger meat and transport it to an orphanage just over the border in Mexico. "We've got about 600 pounds of meat here, Pastor Martensen, but if you don't come get it this morning, we'll have to throw it away." His heart sank. Rollie loved tennis.

Rollie knew what he *wanted* to do. He wanted to play tennis. But he and his seven-year-old daughter piled into their old station wagon with 600 pounds of meat and some other supplies in the back and headed south, the tail end of the car almost scraping the ground from the weight.

When they arrived at the orphanage, the children and nuns raced out to meet them and surrounded the car. "We knew you'd come! We knew you'd come!" they shouted. Rollie thought to himself: "Good heavens, *I* wasn't even sure I was coming. How did they know?" They said, "We ran out of food yesterday, and last night we had a service of prayer and prayed to God for help and for food. We prayed almost the whole night. We knew that God would send you."

On the way home, Rollie's little daughter was uncharacteristically quiet. She said, "Daddy, those children had no food, did they?"

"No, sweetheart, they didn't."

More silence. "God sent us, didn't he, Daddy? God sent us here."

"Yes, honey," he said. "I suppose he did."

In the respective calls of Isaiah (Isa. 6:1-8) and Peter (Luke 5:1–11), a careful reader will soon notice that each has a rather strange encounter with the divine. What you may *not* notice is that neither of them is very excited about that; at least not at first. For all of our modern skepticism and doubt, you'd think a clear revelation from the Lord would be exciting and just the thing to shake a person out of any theological funk or faith stupor.

I recall the wonderful Woody Allen movie titled *Love and Death* in which the main character, Boris, faces a duel at dawn. Boris prays: "God, I'd like to believe in you, to know that you're with me, but could you just give me some sign—just a word, maybe a certain light in a cloud. Anything, Lord. God, if you could just *cough*."

In these two call accounts, God does decidedly more than just cough, yet the reaction from Isaiah and Peter is hardly the "Hallelujah Chorus." The very thing that modern people seek the most—clear and unmistakable "evidence" of the divine—fill future prophet and disciple with dread and fear. Why? (Hint: recall our discussion of the resurrection of the body and God's affirmation of all things physical).

You may already know that Isaiah was a father and a husband before he became a prophet. He was a fairly normal guy who worshiped every week and loved the splendor of the temple there in Jerusalem, the holy city. It was a special place with beautiful architecture, where his family could be sure of meeting God. He probably took the wife and kids there regularly to observe the appointed festivals and went about his business the rest of the week like any other faithful Jewish man.

But this Sabbath was different. And I suppose you can make a case that Isaiah swooned during that worship service because of all the liturgical audio-visuals: singing angels, a mini-earthquake that shook the pillars of the place, holy smoke, and a hot coal, transported with fireplace tongs, touching our hero's lips. It was just too much.

Use your imagination and pick out several elements of our own liturgy in this old story. Expecting bread and wine, maybe you too would faint if your pastor came at your lips with a burning coal. On the receiving end, I think it might be just the thing, actually, to purify the cynical sassiness with which my good wife says I'm perpetually afflicted.

But for my money, it's something else entirely that flushes out Isaiah's angst. I think it's not really *the presence* of these six-winged creatures, but rather *the song they're singing*. It's a song Lutherans sing every week. "Holy, holy, holy is the Lord of hosts; the whole earth is full of his glory" (Isa. 6:3). Please remember that for a guy like Isaiah, this was pretty earth-shaking news. Isaiah knew of God's holiness, no doubt, but the story he knew revealed a fairly *particular* holiness—a tabernacle, a mountain, a temple, a set of laws: a specific, verifiable, locatable God. When these angels started singing about a God who wasn't quite so contained, whose holiness and glory filled the whole earth, whose theological sway affirmed all of creation, then Isaiah could only conclude that there was a great deal of God elsewhere, spilling out into his entire life and week—a God who could show up, well, *anywhere*.

As important as temple worship was (and as vital as Sunday worship in your home congregation *is*), this pattern of worship is not something where one can check off an hourly dose of God for the week and then move on to other things. Part of the important movement from justification to sanctification for a Christian is coming to the realization that God sanctifies and hallows not only a church building and a certain time, but also the entire earth and all time. Worship for Isaiah that day revealed that it was *all* about God—the "whole earth is full" of God; there's not a place or situation or an occupation where God isn't. Is that good news or bad? Well, for Isaiah on that particular Sabbath morning, it absolutely shook his world.

Now I cannot imagine Isaiah heading out to play tennis like Rollie Martensen that morning in southern California, the morning he received the call to pick up hamburger meat for those orphaned kids. But I can imagine Isaiah's fairly normal life being normal no more. Why? Because the soon-to-be prophet could no longer manage and encounter God only in a predictable place. If God fills the whole earth, then Isaiah's day job, as he once knew it, was over.

This was Isaiah's realization that morning: there was not a single facet of his entire life where God would not be showing up. If God fills the whole earth, the whole heretofore happy chasm between sacred and secular becomes quickly bridged. The worship service that morning was teaching Isaiah that God has everything to do with *his whole life*—his job, his hobbies, his bank account, his sexuality, his free time, his vacation, even his private imagination. Do you recall Isaiah's response to this learning? "Woe is me!" cried Isaiah (6:5). Indeed.

Something of Isaiah's anxiety is also occurring in the call of Peter (Luke 5:1-11). You'd think Peter would be as pleased as punch with a boatful of fish. The poor guy's been fishing all night without the slightest nibble. And now he's got so many flopping red snapper that even two boats can't hold the catch. Is Peter happy about this? Does he hug Jesus or dance a little jig, imagining food on the table or coins in the bank? No, on all counts.

Peter falls on his knees (right there in the boat!) and says, "Go away from me, Lord, for I'm a sinful man." It's a fairly cheeky thing to tell Jesus to take a hike. Like Isaiah, Peter now understands that the little curtain between sacred and secular has been forever pulled away. His day job, at least as he once understood it, is over. His fishing business is transformed and he will now "catch people." Peter's kneeling and religious emotion in that boat is significant. He now understands that holiness can no longer find containment in certain sacred times and places. Later in Luke, at the death of Jesus, this same idea is more dramatically conveyed as "the curtain of the temple was torn in two" (Luke 23:45). The Spirit of the Lord, commended to the Father (23:46), the creator, is now loose in the world and fully accessible to all God's people throughout all creation.

Holy, holy, holy is the Lord of hosts. The whole earth is full of your glory. Not just the whole temple. Not just the whole church building. The whole earth.

When those familiar words really sink in, when we realize for the first or 500th time that God fills our whole existence, our every minute and moment, then nothing can ever be compartmentalized again—not our jobs, not our family life, not our down time, not our politics, not our bank accounts or shopping trips; not how we vote or play or love. It *all* has to do with God.

Please don't forget that Isaiah and Peter were normal guys with fairly normal lives. I really don't think it was the paranormal nature of their encounter that changed them. It was the realization that God could no longer be managed or controlled in a specific place.

I spend some time juxtaposing these two call stories with the Easter story from Luke 24 because it's very easy to relegate our notion of resurrection to a specific "spiritual" and "future" place called heaven that is completely removed and separate from our lives here on earth. We believe in a resurrection *of the body*, which includes God's affirmation of the physical—our work-a-day, sexual, bill-paying, child-rearing, dishwashing, lawn-mowing lives. Jesus says, "I *am* the resurrection and the life" (John 11:25, emphasis added). His promise begins now, not just on some shadowy day in the future. There is no facet of this life—on earth or in heaven—that God will not transform and redeem through the sanctifying power of the Holy Spirit. Historian David Steinmetz writes powerfully about this idea:

> Conversion proceeds layer by layer, relationship by relationship, here a little, there a little, until the whole personality, and not merely one side of it, has been recreated by God. Conversion refers not only to the initial moment of faith, no matter how dramatic or revolutionary it may seem, but to the whole life of the believer and the network of

relationships in which that life is entangled: personal, familial, social, economic, political.[3]

When a disciple arrives at an understanding of what the church has long meant by "resurrection of the body," the doctrines of justification and sanctification find an interesting and new intersection. Isaiah ("I am a man of unclean lips") and Peter ("I am a sinful man!") are both acutely aware of their shortcomings and dire need of grace. But neither man is left with that theological realization only. Both are called into a world absolutely infused with the presence of God and sent to other sinners with the good news that God desires to transform the entirety of their normal and daily lives, not just part. I suspect that even Luther would give his catechetical assent that "this is most certainly true."

Questions for Discussion

1. Is the author's description of "the resurrection of the body" new for you? Describe your reaction to this ancient teaching.

2. Name some of the forces in this life that lead us to "compartmentalize" our faith and discipleship.

3. How can your congregation help make more specific connections between Sunday and the rest of the week?

7

Holiness in a Broken World: A New Way of Seeing

"That wafer might as well be a burnt marshmallow for all the passion it evokes in that crowd," my father said one Sunday as we drove home. "If Jesus Christ and his disciples marched in during a service, the ushers would tell them to have a seat, that the congregation would be glad to hear what they had to say as soon as the monthly business meeting was over."[1]

—Ron Rash, *Chemistry and Other Stories*

Twenty-three years out of seminary, I've now participated in hundreds of funerals of people I've come to love. You may think that pastors are somehow immune to the emotional realities of death and dying. To be honest, every time I walk into a room of grieving people it feels as if I'm starting from scratch concerning what to say and do.

I remember a call I got one Saturday afternoon when we lived in the Shenandoah Valley of Virginia. It came from a caring pediatrician who was in the emergency room with some of our church members. Their little boy, Eric, age three, had died suddenly from heart complications that had been with him from birth. It's not easy looking at a little boy whose eyes will not open again, lying still on a table, surrounded by brokenhearted parents who are beyond any comfort at this point—a perfectly formed little child.

I recall an evening and a long, dark night, when a young father and I walked for hours through the halls of a quiet hospital. His wife was in the process of delivering a child they both knew was stillborn after an eight-month pregnancy—some unexplainable complication that came with no warning. The labor and delivery took hours. "Why does God allow this kind of thing?" the faithful and loving father wanted to know as we walked along a corridor. The child was finally delivered near dawn. We spoke her name before God—Savannah. We prayed and held each other for a long time. The nurse took a picture of the little girl wrapped in a blanket in her parents' arms. I came home at first light, broke down myself, and just could not stop crying, sobs shaking my whole body.

There was an article in *The Washington Post* several years ago. The article described a mother who lived in an arid and dry African country. She'd had to bury fourteen children over the years. Fourteen little crosses in her backyard. There was nowhere else to bury them. How do people bear such a sight?

Pastors preside at funerals, stand over freshly dug graves, and often read the following famous passage from Paul's first letter to the church in Corinth: "Death has been swallowed up in victory. Where, O death, is your victory? Where, O death, is your sting?" (1 Cor. 15:54-55). Mourners reflect upon these words amidst acres of tombstones and grave markers. It is an audacious and bold proclamation in the middle of a field that seems to herald the very opposite of what we're hearing.

I once wrote a poem, "Discerning the Body," about a young man in my former congregation who died after a long illness. I'm no poet, but these verses came to me quickly, shortly after arriving home from the hospital. For those of you interested in biblical numerology, the first three stanzas have six lines each (666). The last stanza has seven. Make of that what you will.

I watched a young man die today in ICU.
The shell that was his body failed to breathe
after 33 years of breath.
He was as old as Jesus and
looked like him, too—
thin, gaunt, bearded, knees drawn at the waist.

Diabetes, a ravaged kidney, and half a stomach
produced a prognosis
any 12-year-old could cipher.
"It's a blessing," said the nurses who loved him,
whose intensive care knew precisely what it meant
to be blessed.

But what else was there to say, really?
We prayed. I stared.
Silence. Lots.
And then in the ensuing wait
(his weary parents had just stepped out for lunch),
a buzz, faint but there.

A gnat, persisting against my feeble waves,
foraged for supper—first in a nostril,
then boldly in an open mouth.
I watched, transfixed,
reminded of my own nourishment,
my own life, drawn from
One so young.

Courage and the Unseen

What is God up to in the world today? Why does the Holy One often
seem so veiled and hidden, revealed only in glimpses amidst so much
suffering? What difference could the holiness of God's people, the
church, possibly make in such a world?

The tenth chapter of Daniel contains a very odd story about an
angel who is running late—three full weeks late, to be precise (see Dan.
10:1-14). Exiled and far from home in Babylon, Daniel is in dire need
of assistance. It's a challenge to remain faithful in a foreign land. So
Daniel prays for help. No response. He prays for days, weeks, but still
there is no answer, nothing.

After finally arriving and causing our hero to faint dead away, the
angel taps Daniel on the shoulder, "rouses" him to hands and knees

there on the floor of his apartment, and proceeds to explain the lag time between human prayer and angelic response. The angel is late, as it turns out, because he's been held up in a cosmic wrestling match, detained for twenty-one days (Dan. 10:13) in a titanic struggle with an evil prince in the airspace over Persia. Go figure! For three weeks they wrestle. Take a close look at this strange story and notice how this angel finally gets away. His buddy, Saint Michael, arrives and these two friends hook up in what amounts to a celestial tag-team match. Michael jumps into the ring and proceeds to put a headlock on the Persian whippersnapper. Finally free to travel, the unnamed angel arrives at Daniel's side and quickly explains. "Look, from the first day you prayed, you were heard. And I'm here precisely because of your words. I've just been tied up for three weeks or so in a battle you know nothing about. Sorry."

Our Nicene Creed makes this fantastic claim: "We believe in one God, the Father, the Almighty, maker of heaven and earth, of all that is, *seen and unseen.*" We generally have a hard time with that last word, *unseen.* We'd love to view more, but so often we "see in a mirror, dimly" (1 Cor. 13:12). I love the actual Greek translation of this phrase—"in a riddle." That pretty much describes a lot of my faith life. We eventually will see "face to face," but a lot of life is riddles for now. Humans know a great deal about the physical world and the cosmos through which we spin. But so much remains beyond our vision.

To push the metaphor from the book of Daniel even further, maybe the answers to our own prayers and questions are delayed for twenty-one days or twenty-one months or twenty-one years or even twenty-one centuries because of forces and complex dynamics at work that even God cannot fully unravel with the twitch of a nose. "Do not fear, Daniel, for from the *first day* that you set your mind to gain understanding and to humble yourself before your God, your words have been heard, *and I have come because of your words.*"

We sometimes give up on prayer and the ways of Christ because neither prayer nor following Jesus seems workable, functional, dare we say, "successful," in a world like ours. In a world of cancer, terrorism, and unspeakable evil, prayer is fine, really, for suckers who live with their eyes closed, but if you're smart you better have a back-up plan with some real punch to it. That's the conventional wisdom, anyway.

Early Christians believed that Christ conquered unspeakable evil once and for all through the paradox and power of the cross. Using graphic metaphorical language, the book of Revelation describes that cosmic victory over evil. Take a good look at the claim in Rev. 12:11: "They have conquered him [that is, ultimate evil] by the blood of the Lamb and by the word of their testimony, for they did not cling to life even in the face of death." Did you catch that? Evil is overcome by the blood of Jesus and the word. By word and by sacrament. Good news for Lutherans! Relying on such unlikely weapons in the face of such great evil, there is no need to cling to, protect, and fearfully guard our lives *even in the face of death*. Why? Because Christ ultimately has the upper hand even if there seems to be evidence to the contrary. "They did not cling to life."

There is much at stake in being a disciple of Jesus. The world encourages us to believe that life consists of X number of years, time we can see and control and verify, and that's it. Death is the ultimate enemy and death is the end of life. If this is true, then death is the very thing we'll fear and resist and attempt to control the most. We will indeed "cling to life" because, in truth, we might fear that the whole Christian story is just that: a nice story but one needing some real help and "oomph" in a dark world like ours.

But if death is not the end, if death is a passage to life in a realm where we live eternally with the Lamb, how might that translate into how we look at life and death right now? Jesus tells his disciples, "See, I have given you authority to tread on snakes and scorpions, and over all the power of the enemy; *and nothing will hurt you*" (Luke 10:19, emphasis added). Isn't that our promise, too? That in Christ nothing can get us? Believe that, really believe it, and I suspect we'll live differently here on earth. There is more to the kingdom than what we can see.

If evil is indeed conquered by the blood of the Lamb—both historically and with Christ's real presence in the Eucharist—if nothing at all can hurt us, and if an unseen world indeed awaits us, how then shall we now live?

For Now, Glimpses

One Monday afternoon several years ago, I was driving along some-where and found myself thinking about a boy I knew in elementary school in Tennessee. Three other friends and I used to pick on Steve unmercifully. We called him names and used to poke fun at him because he was fat and dumpy and a little nerdy. I'm not proud of that; children can be mean and we were mean to Steve. We even got called into the principal's office once and were told to knock it off.

Well, I hadn't seen or thought about Steve in thirty years or more, and I don't know why I was thinking of him that Monday. Maybe something was unresolved in my conscience. The following Thursday I went to a ministerial association meeting at a local restaurant. I went up and introduced myself to our guest speaker. He paused a second and then said, "Frank Honeycutt." And then he repeated my name. "Are you from Chattanooga by any chance?" he asked. And at that moment I knew. It was Steve from my childhood. He was grown and had a beard, but here he was in this little Virginia town, many hours north of where we grew up. I had not seen him since my cruel antics in the sixth grade. And here we were eating lunch together as grown-ups.

Now what was that all about? And why was I thinking of this boy from my past just three days before our meeting? Was it just random chance? Maybe. Maybe not. *Peek-a-boo.*

Theologian and writer Frederick Buechner describes a visit he took to the home of a friend who recently had died—a friend who died quickly with no chance for good-byes. Buechner and his wife were checking on his friend's widow. They went up to bed after a long con-versation. I'll let him tell the story:

> [That night] I had a short dream about him. I dreamed he was stand-ing there in the dark guest room where we were asleep, looking very much himself in the navy blue jersey and white slacks he often wore. I told him how much we had missed him and how glad I was to see him again. . . . Then I said, "Are you really there, Dudley?" I meant was he there in fact, in truth, or was I merely dreaming he was. His

answer was that he was really there. . . . Then he plucked a strand of wool out of his jersey and tossed it to me. I caught it between my thumb and forefinger, and the feel of it was so palpably real that it woke me up. . . . I told the dream at breakfast the next morning, and I'd hardly finished when my wife spoke. She said she'd seen the strand on the carpet as she was getting dressed. She was sure it hadn't been there the night before. I rushed upstairs to see for myself, and there it was—a little tangle of navy blue wool.[2]

Now, come on. What was that, really? Just a coincidence? Perhaps wish fulfillment? Maybe. Maybe not. *Peek-a-boo.*

Three disciples go on a hike with Jesus (Mark 9:2-8). It was six days after Jesus' rebuke of Peter. Six days after Jesus laid Peter out in the shade. Six days after Jesus clearly spelled out the shape of his mission. Six days after Jesus spoke of denial and cross-bearing and the secret of finding life through losing it. It was frankly a lot for the disciples to digest all at once. Maybe the reference to "six days" in the story is an innocuous reference to time, but in the Bible, six is a number suggesting incompleteness, that which is partial. It's one less than seven, that favorite biblical number pointing to wholeness and perfection. So the number 666, for example, everyone's favorite horrific citation from the book of Revelation, is mainly the author's way of describing "incompleteness" in spades.

Anyway, "six days later" they go on a hike. I've no doubt this little junket was a refreshing break for the disciples from the serious side of Jesus. They hike up and further up, 9,200 feet above sea level, if this is indeed Mount Hermon as many suspect—that's a couple thousand feet higher than our tallest eastern peaks. If that's where these four hiked, then they were higher than Mount Mitchell in North Carolina, for example, or Mount Washington in New Hampshire. It's very possible that they dealt with a bit of ice and snow on top.

But you know what else they saw; stuff that could easily be drawn right out of *The X-Files.* Two Old Testament hall-of-famers (Moses and Elijah) stand there calmly chatting with Jesus as if waiting for a tee time. Mark refuses to say what they were talking about up there.

But even if the disciples are out of earshot, they actually see quite a bit. Peter was so excited that he wanted to build three monuments and erect a memorial park. It would have been a welcome change from listening to his Lord talk like a candidate for the asylum. But then it was over. Just like that. They get a glimpse of the future or certainly something grand. The veil is pulled back, but only for a moment. They wander off the mountain in ordered silence, surely wondering what this was all about. Now why would Jesus lead them up there to see that? *Peek-a-boo.*

What are we to make of premonitions like meeting a classmate I once terrorized in elementary school? What credence can we place in strange dreams where the world to come seems to spill over into this world? What is the purpose of this paranormal hike with Jesus who gives his disciples a glimpse, a peek into the future, but nothing more? Jesus tells his disciples not to talk about what they saw. Scholars have a lot of theories about why he told them to keep mum, but I have a feeling he may have been mostly afraid that others would misunderstand not only his mission but also call into question the sanity of these disciples. I wish I had a dollar in my pastoral work for the number of times people have said to me, "I know you're not going to believe this. I know you're gonna think I'm crazy." Poet Luci Shaw says, "It's a cracked, crossover world, waiting / for bridges."[3] If we keep our eyes open, we'll stop calling these bridges "luck" or "chance" or "coincidence."

For some reason, however, God only allows us to see so far in this life. There are limits to our view. Maybe if the curtain separating present and future was completely lifted back, we would be blinded by the divine glory, and God knows this. The Bible says that Moses knew the Lord "face to face" but maybe such a full-frontal encounter would obliterate our humanity, completely wiping out who we are. So we are mostly given glimpses. We worship a God who only seems to flirt with us—a sign here and there, consistent but sometimes veiled messages from another world to this one. The Nicene Creed says it well: "We believe in all things seen and unseen."

These glimpses are more than psychological carrots on a stick for people mired in great suffering and poverty; for a world that resorts so quickly to violence and force and shelves the teachings of Jesus in favor of more "practical" solutions.

Six days later, Jesus led them up a high mountain apart. Six days. We live in an incomplete six-day world, awaiting the complete fulfillment of the seventh day. For now, we receive snatches of insight and inspiration. This is the nature of sanctification on this side of the grave. On a mountain, in a dream, in a restaurant, or kneeling at an altar for a bit of bread and wine, pointing to a great and glorious feast—we are dealing with a Lord who longs to reveal his glory to us, who longs to illumine our struggles in a world mingled for now with both light and shadow.

Questions for Discussion

1. Read closely the story in Dan. 10:1-14 and (within the context of the narrative) discuss your understanding of the nature of prayer.

2. Describe a "coincidence" or "chance event" in your life that may have been something more.

3. Reflect upon this line from Luci Shaw: "It's a cracked, crossover world, waiting / for bridges."

Afterword: Fishing Naked

Somewhere Lutheran theologian Martin Marty makes the excellent point that living the Christian life is like walking a tightrope that stretches precariously between two compelling theological pitfalls: cheap grace (see James 2:14-17) on one side and works righteousness (see Rom 3:27-28) on the other. Our proper place, he says, is to maintain the tension on the tightrope and try to walk there.

In this book I have tried to heighten the tension described by Marty. Many Lutherans are understandably uncomfortable with any talk about sanctification, suspecting that all such reflection easily leads to a false compromise of our Reformation heritage. We all know sanctimonious individuals like Count Olaf in *Lemony Snicket's A Series of Unfortunate Events*. In the movie version of this story, Jim Carrey plays Count Olaf who tries to warp the minds of the three Baudelaire children: "You know," says the snide count, "there's a big world out there, filled with desperate orphans who would gladly swim across an ocean of thumbtacks just to be eclipsed by the long shadow that is cast by my accomplishments." I am well aware of the danger here. One can become so proud of personal piety that it's easy to lapse into judgment of others who don't seem to be on the same spiritual plane. The old story of the tax collector and the Pharisee (Luke 18:9-14) quickly comes to mind: "God," prays the proud man, "I thank you that I am not like other people." He confidently lists his spiritual accomplishments. There is much in the man that's commendable. What pastor does not long for a congregation of people who take seriously both tithing *and* fasting? But only one of these two who pray to God that morning in worship goes home "justified" (v. 14), according to Jesus, and it's not the guy who engages regularly in spiritual practices.

Having participated in conversations with Lutheran pastors who have accused me of actually being something else, I realize that many "orthodox" Lutherans may not like what I've written here. Even so, my hope is that these words will spark conversation about sanctification without lapsing into the pious sanctimony of Count Olaf and the proud Pharisee. And so I close with a favorite narrative (John 21:1-14) centering on Peter, whose rather mercurial discipleship was always a work in progress. His lapses are my (our) own and reveal that the Holy Spirit is never finished with any of us. Allow me to put on my Perry Mason sleuthing hat and do a little biblical investigative work, a little forensic probing, as we examine the curious story of Saint Peter fishing in the nude.

Saint Peter with His Pants Down

Have you ever noticed the number of disciples piled into Peter's den that night just before they all shoved off to cast their nets? By my count, there are seven of them (John 21:2) kicked back there, wondering what to do next. We know about the demise of Judas, but this leaves four disciples unaccounted for. Without saying so directly, this may be a little scribal tip-off that it was hard to hold the community together in those days just after Easter. Any pastor is familiar with crowds that flock to worship on Easter Sunday and then mysteriously vanish. Even the early Christians seemed to have something of a problem with ecclesiastical letdown and even disappointment in the days just after our Lord's resurrection.

So the seven guys are sitting there long before the advent of cable television, twiddling their thumbs, no doubt talking like a bunch of guys often do, maybe playing canasta or Parcheesi. But I really get the feeling they're all just a little bored. There's no way of really knowing this, of course, but when Peter finally says, *"I am going fishing,"* I sense that he's decided to head out into the night not because he needs the money, but because there's nothing better to do.

Remember: these erstwhile casters of nets were *not supposed to be out fishing* at this point in their lives, at least not for the wiggly swimmers they once chased, right? Jesus clearly called these men[1] to leave their nets, to go out and share the gospel, to engage in a different sort of fishing. So as day breaks there on the water, it's worth at least a bit of our time to try to determine the tone of voice used by this stranger on the beach. We know who is standing there; these seven haven't a clue. "Children, you have no fish, have you?" Now, wonder with me just a second. How do you think the man standing there in the mist in the early light offered those words? It's hard to say. I'd like to think he was patient with his students, but I would not be surprised to hear a bit of an edge in his voice either, a sarcastic hint that does not register right at first. "Children, you haven't caught a thing, have you?" Translation: *What in the heck are you doing out here?*

Ultimately, just to fool with them a bit I'd say, the nets are filled with so many fish that the seven disciples can't begin to haul the catch in. I'm reminded of that strange scene in the book of Numbers where God finally responds to the ungrateful and disobedient Israelites who don't really like their new life there in the desert. They want their old life back. So God says, "You want meat? Okay, I'll give you all the meat you want. I'll give you people meat until it's coming out of your nostrils!"[2]

The fish are jumping, there's a guy on the beach talking funny, and here's where we get a glimpse of our hero in all his glory. For some odd reason, Saint Peter has been fishing in the buff all this time. Maybe it was hot that night. Maybe fishermen in the first century did this all the time so that their clothes wouldn't get tangled in the nets. I'm not really sure. I do know that John, the author of this Gospel, does not waste ink on this sort of detail. For John, it means *something*.

Peter, in the buff, finally recognizes who's talking there on the beach. But watch what he does. He pulls on his pants and jumps into the water. Now isn't that weird? If Peter *isn't supposed* to be fishing, if he's supposed to be doing something else entirely, then Peter really may not be reacting in joy—*Golly gee, it's Jesus! Praise the Lord!* No, Peter may react oddly because he's been caught, caught, in truth, with his pants down.

Do you recall another naked guy in the Bible who put on some clothes after he got caught? Think of a long-ago garden, a tree, and a serpent. Think of a young couple in hiding, once naked, now (after their disobedience) wearing a new wardrobe of fig leaves when God strolls by. Perhaps John wants us to think of this old story from Genesis as this fisherman dons trousers and jumps in the drink. Although I have no evidence from the sacramental tradition to substantiate this hunch, I'm also wondering if our ancient practice of donning a baptismal garment as water is poured from a flowing font finds connection with this odd fishing posture. Peter has been caught (like Adam and Eve before him) in his disobedience. He's caught off guard—just caught, period, when he's supposed to be doing something else entirely.

In Lake Tahoe, there's a gambling casino with a bar where the only women's room is at the top of a long flight of stairs. A person climbs the stairs in full view of the crowded occupants of the bar, enters the restroom, closes the door, and notices a piece of art hanging on one wall. The painting is a tasteful picture of a man wearing nothing but a strategically-located fig leaf. The curious thing about this picture is that the fig leaf is hinged, lift-able. You can probably guess where this story is going. Restroom users who are curious enough to peek under this hinged fig leaf set off a series of bells, whistles, and lights in the bar below. The restroom user, of course, then emerges to a standing ovation and descends the stairs in what is no doubt one of longest walks of her life.[3]

If this old story is at least partly about *getting caught* doing something you're not supposed to do—being discovered by a God "from whom no secrets are hid"—it's important to note closely the gospel behavior of this man on the beach. Are there pointed reprimands waiting for Peter and these seven? Lectures about what they're supposed to be doing instead of fishing? Stern sermons about disobedience and disappointment?

Notably, there is none of this there on the beach. Instead, there is breakfast. And there is a Eucharistic pattern of words that none of us should miss. "Jesus came and took the bread and gave it to them, and did the same with the fish." *In the night in which he was betrayed, he took the bread, gave thanks, broke it, and gave it to the disciples.*

We live in a world where humans engage in behavior that brings God great disappointment. We live in a world of great fear and suspicion. We live upon a planet that we are slowly choking with our waste and excessive lifestyles. We harbor silly grudges against one another and treat people shabbily on a daily basis. We know the teachings of Jesus (we are his disciples, after all), and somehow we pretend that he could not have really meant what he said. I can only imagine how God must feel upon watching us behave the way we do. How much divine restraint must be inherent in the gift of human freedom and trust and how angry the Creator must be.

But then I think of this scene on the beach. And suddenly, hundreds of people are there, not just these seven disciples. Thousands, a numberless throng—all of us, each of us, *caught*; caught doing something when we know better. I wait for the hammer to fall. I wait for the words of disappointment and judgment. But four words interrupt whatever I'm expecting; four words travel across time and space and nationality and planetary challenge and obvious guilty reality. He took the bread, broke it, gave thanks, and said something we'd never expect in a million years: *Come and have breakfast.*

And you know what? The words are just enough to break my heart and drive me to my knees. The words empower and equip me to be a better person, a better husband, father, friend, and citizen of this earth. They create a new world with new possibilities. Four words offered to the wayward; all who've been caught—naked and guilty.

"Come," he says. "Come and have breakfast." We jump into the watery sea of grace and swim ashore.

Notes

Introduction

1. Flannery O'Connor, "Revelation," in *The Complete Stories of Flannery O'Connor* (New York: Farrar, Straus and Giroux, 1984), 491.

2. Robert Kolb and Timothy J. Wengert, eds., *The Book of Concord: The Confessions of the Evangelical Lutheran Church* (Minneapolis: Fortress Press, 2000), 380.

3. Kolb and Wengert, eds., *The Book of Concord*, 385.

4. Barbara Brown Taylor, *Speaking of Sin: The Lost Language of Salvation* (Boston: Cowley Publications, 2000), 86.

5. Donald L. Alexander, ed., *Christian Spirituality: Five Views of Sanctification* (Downers Grove, Ill.: InterVarsity, 1988), 13, 22–23.

Chapter 1

1. Robert Kolb and Timothy J. Wengert, eds., *The Book of Concord: The Confessions of the Evangelical Lutheran Church* (Minneapolis: Fortress Press, 2000), 360.

2. See Mark 1:9-13 and Matt. 3:13—4:11.

3. Bill Wylie Kellerman, ed., *A Keeper of the Word: Selected Writings of William Stringfellow* (Grand Rapids, Mich.: Eerdmans, 1994), 312, 314. The emphasis here is Stringfellow's.

4. Bryan Stone, *Evangelism after Christendom: The Theology and Practice of Christian Witness* (Grand Rapids, Mich.: Brazos, 2007), 259.

5. I am paraphrasing here from Mal. 3:1-3.

Chapter 2

1. David James Duncan, *The Brothers K* (New York: Bantam Books, 1992), 61.

2. See James 2:1-4.

3. Robert Kolb and Timothy J. Wengert, eds., *The Book of Concord: The Confessions of the Evangelical Lutheran Church* (Minneapolis: Fortress Press, 2000), 617.

Chapter 3

1. Dallas Willard, *The Spirit of the Disciplines: Understanding How God Changes Lives* (San Francisco: HarperCollins, 1991), 8.

2. Bryan Stone, *Evangelism after Christendom: The Theology and Practice of Christian Witness* (Grand Rapids, Mich.: Brazos, 2007), 78. The emphasis here is Stone's.

3. I am indebted here to Dallas Willard who says, "Grace is not opposed to effort, it is opposed to earning." See Dallas Willard, *The Great Omission: Reclaiming Jesus' Essential Teachings on Discipleship* (San Francisco: HarperCollins, 2006), 61.

4. Peter J. Gomes, *The Good Book: Reading the Bible with Mind and Heart* (New York: William Morrow, 1996), 6.

5. Southern Poverty Law Center, www.splcenter.org (accessed January 23, 2008).

Chapter 4

1. Anthony Doerr, *About Grace* (New York: Penguin Books, 2004), 360.

2. C. S. Lewis, *The Screwtape Letters* (New York: Bantam, 1982), 23.

3. Robert Kolb and Timothy J. Wengert, eds., *The Book of Concord: The Confessions of the Evangelical Lutheran Church* (Minneapolis: Fortress Press, 2000), 439.

4. Eugene Peterson, *The Message: The Bible in Contemporary Language* (Colorado Springs: NavPress, 2004).

Chapter 5

1. Reynolds Price, *The Good Priest's Son* (New York: Scribner and Sons, 2005), 110.

2. Wendy Kaminer, *Sleeping with Extra-Terrestrials: The Rise of Irrationalism and Perils of Piety* (New York: Pantheon Books, 1999), 25.

3. Ron Allen, "Resisting the Powers" in Jana Childers, ed., *Purposes of Preaching* (St. Louis: Chalice, 2004), 29.

Chapter 6

1. David Yeago, "Martin Luther on Renewal and Sanctification: *Simil Iustus et Peccator* Revisited" in *Sapere teologico e unita della fede: Studi in onore del Prof. Jared Wicks* (Rome, Italy: Editrice Pontificia Universita Gregoriana, 2004), 656–657.

2. The following section on the resurrection of the body first appeared in my article, "Bones for a New Day" in *The Lutheran* (April 2007): 24–26. Used here with permission.

3. David C. Steinmetz, "Reformation and Conversion" in *Theology Today* (April 1978): 30.

Chapter 7

1. Ron Rash, "Chemistry" in *Chemistry and Other Stories* (New York: Picador, 2007), 27.

2. Frederick Buechner, *The Clown in the Belfry: Writings on Faith and Fiction* (New York: HarperCollins, 1992), 7–8.

3. Luci Shaw, "Ghostly" in *Writing the River* (Colorado Springs: Pinon, 1994), 37.

Afterword

1. John 20:21-23; Matt. 28:16-20; Luke 5:1-11.

2. Num. 11:19-20.

3. The story is adapted from an article by Martin E. Marty in *The Christian Century* (April 1, 1992): 351.

For Further Reading

Alexander, Donald L., ed. *Christian Spirituality: Five Views of Sanctification*. Downers Grove, Ill.: InterVarsity, 1988.

Guder, Darrell L. *The Continuing Conversion of the Church*. Grand Rapids, Mich.: Eerdmans, 2000.

Honeycutt, Frank G. *Preaching for Adult Conversion and Commitment: Invitation to a Life Transformed*. Nashville: Abingdon, 2003.

Lewis, C. S. *The Screwtape Letters*. New York: Bantam Books, 1982.

Mathewes-Green, Frederica. *The Illumined Heart: The Ancient Path of Transformation*. Brewster, Mass.: Paraclete, 2001.

Nouwen, Henri J.M. *Life of the Beloved: Spiritual Living in a Secular World*. New York: Crossroad Publishing Company, 1992.

Winner, Lauren F. *Real Sex: The Naked Truth about Chastity*. Grand Rapids, Mich.: Brazos, 2005.